DISEASES AND DISORDERS

LIVING WITH ALLERGIES

By Juliana Burkhart

Portions of this book originally appeared in *Allergies* by Barbara Sheen.

LUCENT PRESS

Published in 2019 by
Lucent Press, an Imprint of Greenhaven Publishing, LLC
353 3rd Avenue
Suite 255
New York, NY 10010

Designer: Andrea Davison-Bartolotta
Editor: Jennifer Lombardo

Library of Congress Cataloging-in-Publication Data

Names: Burkhart, Juliana, author.
Title: Living with allergies / Juliana Burkhart.
Description: New York : Lucent, [2019] | Series: Diseases and disorders | Includes bibliographical references and index.
Identifiers: LCCN 2018017841 (print) | LCCN 2018018352 (ebook) | ISBN 9781534564848 (eBook) | ISBN 9781534564831 (library bound book) | ISBN 9781534564824 (pbk. book)
Subjects: LCSH: Allergy–Juvenile literature.
Classification: LCC RC584 (ebook) | LCC RC584 .B86 2019 (print) | DDC 616.97/3–dc23
LC record available at https://lccn.loc.gov/2018017841

Printed in the United States of America

CPSIA compliance information: Batch #BW19KL: For further information contact Greenhaven Publishing LLC, New York, New York, at 1-844-317-7404.

Please visit our website, www.greenhavenpublishing.com. For a free color catalog of all our high-quality books, call toll free 1-844-317-7404 or fax 1-844-317-7405.

CONTENTS

FOREWORD

Illness is an unfortunate part of life, and it is one that is often misunderstood. Thanks to advances in science and technology, people have been aware for many years that diseases such as the flu, pneumonia, and chicken pox are caused by viruses and bacteria. These diseases all cause physical symptoms that people can see and understand, and many people have dealt with these diseases themselves. However, sometimes diseases that were previously unknown in most of the world turn into epidemics and spread across the globe. Without an awareness of the method by which these diseases are spread—through the air, through human waste or fluids, through sexual contact, or by some other method—people cannot take the proper precautions to prevent further contamination. Panic often accompanies epidemics as a result of this lack of knowledge.

Knowledge is power in the case of mental disorders, as well. Mental disorders are just as common as physical disorders, but due to a lack of awareness among the general public, they are often stigmatized. Scientists have studied them for years and have found that they are generally caused by hormonal imbalances in the brain, but they have not yet determined with certainty what causes those imbalances or how to fix them. Because even mild mental illness is stigmatized in Western society, many people prefer not to talk about it.

Chronic pain disorders are also not well understood—even by researchers—and do not yet have foolproof treatments. People who have a mental disorder or a disease or disorder that causes them to feel chronic pain can be the target of uninformed opinions. People who do not have these disorders sometimes struggle to understand how difficult it can be to deal with the symptoms. These disorders are often termed "invisible illnesses" because no one can see the symptoms; this leads many people to doubt that they exist or are serious problems. Additionally, people who have an undiagnosed disorder may understand that they are experiencing the world in a different way than their peers, but they have no one to turn to for answers.

Misinformation about all kinds of ailments is often spread through personal anecdotes, social media, and even news sources. This series aims to present accurate information about both physical and mental conditions so young adults will have a better understanding of them. Each volume discusses the symptoms of a particular disease or disorder, ways it is currently being treated, and the research that is being done to understand it further. Advice for people who may be suffering from the disorder is included, as well as information for their loved ones about how best to support them.

With fully cited quotes, a list of recommended books and websites for further research, and informational charts, this series provides young adults with a factual introduction to common illnesses. By learning more about these ailments, they will be better able to prevent the spread of contagious diseases, show compassion to people who are dealing with invisible illnesses, and take charge of their own health.

A LIFE-THREATENING PROBLEM

"Anaphylaxis." Ellie, age six, stumbles over the pronunciation of the word. "I am anaphylactic to egg, peanut, tree nuts, and sesame." Anaphylaxis is a life-threatening allergic reaction. If Ellie accidentally eats any of the foods she is allergic to, or if her food comes into contact with one of her allergens, she experiences a severe reaction. "I am always careful about what I eat. Every meal. Every snack. Every day. I always carry my epinephrine. I never know when I might have an emergency."[1] Even with prompt treatment by an injection of epinephrine, a hormonal medication, she could still end up in the hospital.

Ellie is one of millions of Americans who suffer from allergies. A severe allergy can disrupt life at home, school, and work, and it can limit travel. Allergy sufferers experience a wide range of symptoms, severity, and triggering allergens.

More Than Seasonal Sniffles

It is widely believed that allergies are seasonal nuisances, causing no more trouble than the common cold. The unfortunate truth is that allergic reactions can lead to hospitalization or even death.

Even when allergy cases do not require hospitalization or threaten lives, they do produce unpleasant symptoms that can make allergy sufferers feel unwell, worsen other health conditions, or cause

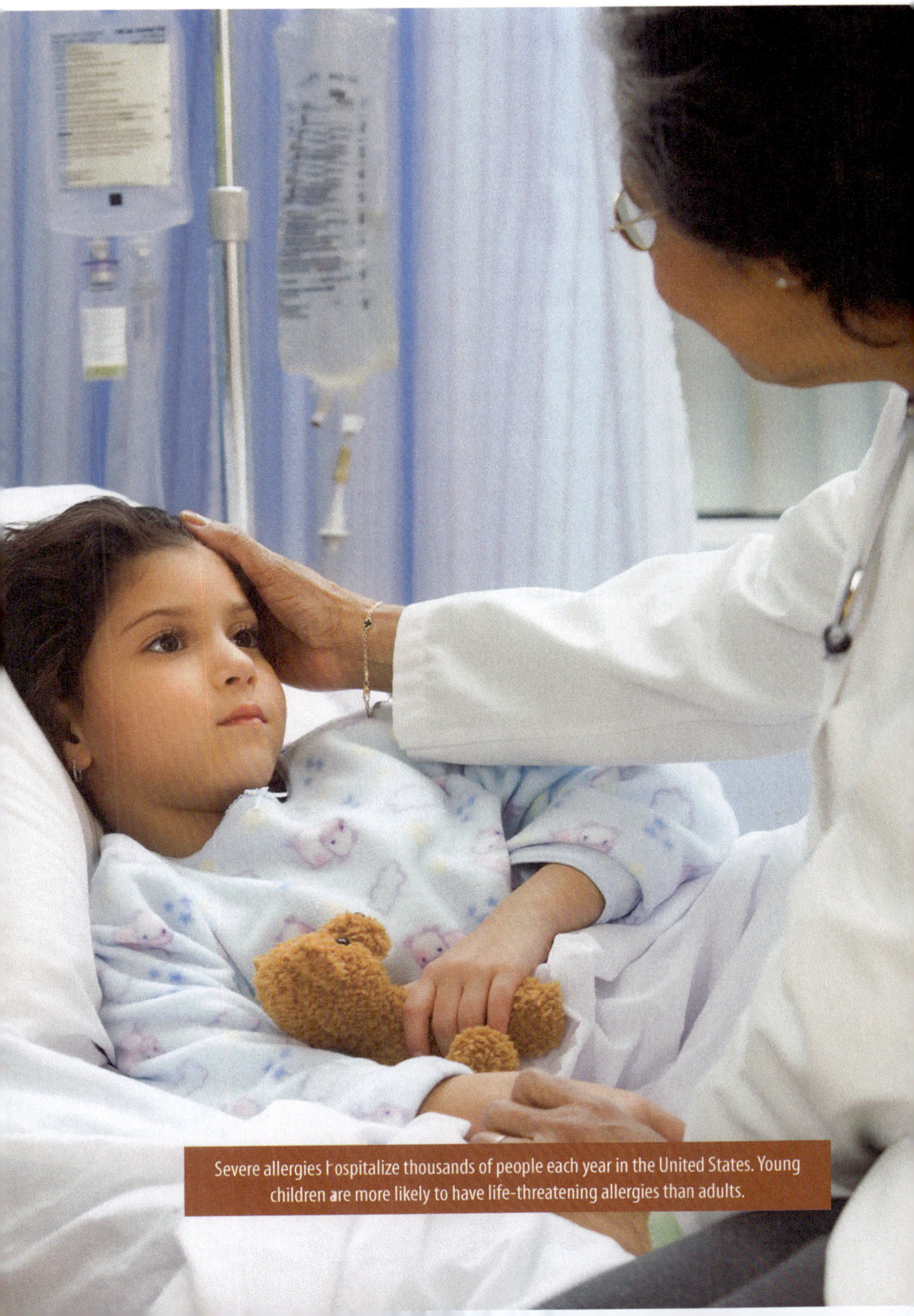

Severe allergies hospitalize thousands of people each year in the United States. Young children are more likely to have life-threatening allergies than adults.

secondary illnesses to develop. In some instances, allergies—especially those to food, insect venom, and medications—can be deadly.

Making matters worse, the number of people throughout the world with allergies has been on the rise for decades. According to Dr. Scott H. Sicherer of Mount Sinai Hospital in New York City, "We're basically looking at what may be a public-health crisis."[2]

Currently, an estimated 50 million people in the United States have allergies. That translates to more than 15 percent of all Americans. Roughly 20 percent of all Europeans are allergy sufferers, too—and these numbers are growing. According to the European Academy of Allergy and Clinical Immunology, emergency room visits for severe allergic reactions increased by 700 percent between 2001 and 2011.

A 2005 study conducted jointly by the National Institute of Environmental Health Sciences and the National Institute of Allergy and Infectious Diseases showed how vulnerable people are to allergies. Researchers exposed the skin of 10,500 individuals between the ages of 6 and 59 to the 10 most common allergens—normally harmless substances, such as pollen or dust, that cause some people to experience allergic reactions—then measured their reactions. Fifty-four percent of the subjects were sensitive to at least one allergen. This means that more than half the subjects were already allergic to at least one allergen or were at risk of developing such an allergy in the future. The scientists said the test looked at only 10 out of thousands of potential allergens, and if the subjects had been exposed to more allergens, the reaction rate would probably have been quite a bit higher. Since the subjects represented a cross section of typical Americans, if all the people in the United States were tested in the same way, the results would be similar. Interestingly, when the same test was conducted

30 years earlier, only 27 percent of the subjects reacted, which is an indicator of how vulnerability to allergies has increased.

Impact on Society

Because the incidence of allergies is so high, the condition has a substantial impact on society. It burdens the health care system, decreases work and school productivity, and negatively affects the quality of life of allergy sufferers. According to the Centers for Disease Control and Prevention (CDC), allergies are the 6th leading cause of chronic illness in Americans, costing $18 billion each year in doctor's visits, medications, and emergency services.

Allergies also cause absenteeism in students and workers. American students miss approximately 2 million school days each year due to allergies. That translates to 10,000 absences per day. American workers miss 1.8 million workdays annually due to allergies.

Even when students and workers go to school or work on days when they are suffering from allergy symptoms, their symptoms impair their ability to function well, causing their productivity to drop significantly. According to allergy specialist Dr. Richard Page of Garland, Texas, people with allergies "have less energy, and difficulty concentrating."[3] Additionally, a common side effect of many allergy medications is drowsiness, which raises safety concerns in the workplace.

Educating Others

In light of the considerable impact allergies have on individuals and society, it is not sensible or safe to dismiss allergies as simply an annoyance. By learning ways to manage and control their allergies, individuals with allergies can improve the quality of their lives. When friends, family members, and coworkers learn more about allergies, they know how to provide allergy sufferers with appropriate support. In some cases, such knowledge can be a lifesaver. Alyssa, who has a severe milk allergy, put it this way: "People without allergies should be knowledgeable on the signs of a reaction, know the different medications, and know how to help. If more non-allergic people understood … allergies, they would be more likely to help when an allergic person has a reaction."[4]

CHAPTER ONE

WHAT CAUSES ALLERGIES?

An allergy is a hypersensitivity disorder. Allergic individuals are overly sensitive to one or more allergens, which are normally harmless substances that do not cause problems in most other people. This sensitivity causes their immune system to overreact, producing symptoms such as itchy skin, watery eyes, rashes, nausea, and hives. Anaphylaxis, or anaphylactic shock, is a condition in which the immune system severely overreacts to the allergen, causing blood pressure to drop suddenly. The throat and airways may close, making it impossible for the victim to breathe. Without immediate treatment, anaphylactic shock can cause death. Common allergens include pollen, mold, pet dander, insect venom, latex, drugs, and many foods, to name just a few. These allergens can be found in homes, schools, and workplaces. Individuals who suffer from serious allergies must be careful about coming into contact with their allergens.

Immune System Response

The immune system consists of billions of specialized cells that protect the body from harmful foreign substances, such as bacteria, viruses, fungi, and parasites. Through a series of steps called an immune response, the immune system determines the identity of a foreign invader, establishes whether it is harmful, and then, if the invader is identified as a threat, launches an attack against it.

Persistent health problems can sometimes be explained when mold is found hidden in damp corners of the home or office.

When a foreign substance—a molecule of a material the body does not recognize—enters the body, white blood cells called lymphocytes are sent to the area. When they come into contact with the invader, they surround it. Proteins on the surface of the foreign substance stick to the lymphocytes, and the composition of the proteins alerts the immune system to the identity of the invader.

If the invader is identified as an antigen—a dangerous foreign substance, such as a poison, bacteria, or virus—the immune system releases specialized proteins known as antibodies. The body produces millions of different antibodies, each shaped to match up with and lock on to a specific antigen. When an antibody locks on to an antigen, it releases powerful chemicals that destroy the antigen. However, the first time the body is exposed to a particular antigen, it takes about two weeks for the immune system to manufacture the appropriate antibodies. Thereafter, the immune system is always on guard against that particular antigen. Normally, this is how the body builds resistance to illnesses.

In the case of allergies, the immune system mistakenly identifies a harmless substance, such as grass pollen, for a dangerous invader. The first time the body is exposed to that allergen, the immune system begins manufacturing an antibody known as immunoglobulin E (IgE). As with all antibody production, it takes the immune system at least two weeks to produce the specific IgE antibody that matches the allergen.

Once the antibody is produced, it attaches to mast cells. These are cells that line the nose, throat, lungs, skin, and gastrointestinal tract, the areas of the body in which allergens settle. The next time the allergen enters the body, IgE locks on to it. This activates the mast cells, triggering the release of chemicals contained within them. This process is known as allergic sensitization.

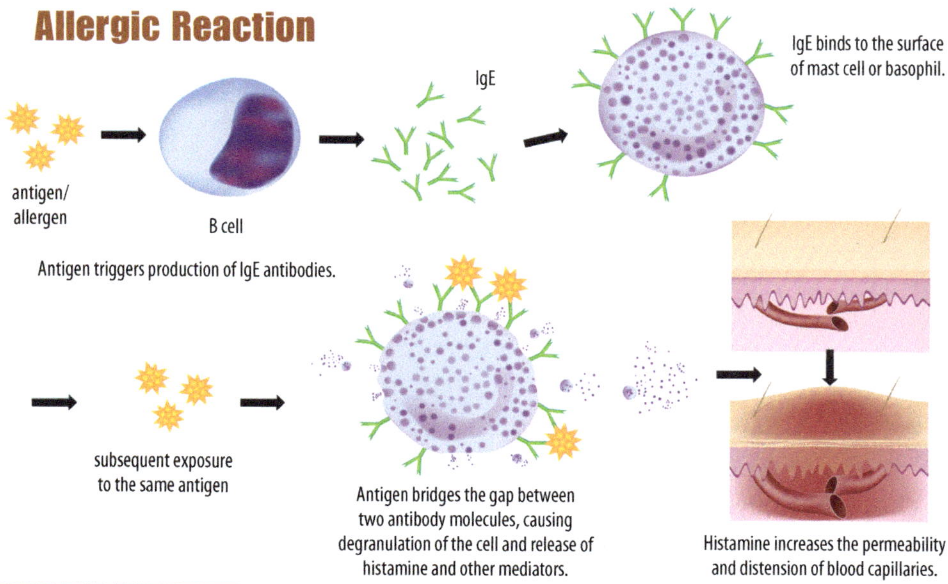

When an allergen enters the body, the immune system mistakenly identifies it as a harmful substance and produces IgE antibodies to defend against it.

A Chain Reaction

Histamine is one of the chemicals the mast cells release. The release of histamine causes inflammation, which is one of the body's ways of fighting harmful organisms. However, when no actual threat to the body exists, as in the case of allergies, inflammation sets off a chain of events that causes problems. First, in order to get blood and immune cells to the affected area, inflammation causes blood vessels to widen. As a result, blood floods into the affected area, causing redness. As blood and immune cells leak into nearby tissues, swelling develops. When swollen tissues press on nearby nerve endings, irritation, itching, or pain develops. Authors Dr. Frank K. Kwong and Bruce W. Cook described what happens when an inhaled allergen triggers an allergic reaction in the nose: "The substance histamine will cause the rich supply of blood vessels in the nose to become leaky. Imagine many

The Body's Defense System

The immune system is the body's defense system against disease. White blood cells are the key to this system. There are many types of white blood cells. They work together to fight harmful microorganisms. Each has a specific job.

Neutrophils are the most common type of white blood cell. Their job is to fight bacteria. Dead neutrophils are what make up pus, which is the thick, yellowish fluid in a pimple or other infected tissue.

Eosinophils and basophils are less common. Eosinophils attack parasites in the skin and the lungs. Basophils are involved in causing inflammation.

Lymphocytes focus on viruses and bacteria. There are two types of lymphocytes: T cells and B cells. B cells produce antibodies. T cells identify antigens and signal the release of antibodies. Along with antibodies, T cells attack the threatening substance. In the case of allergies, the T cells misidentify a harmless substance as a dangerous antigen and attack it accordingly.

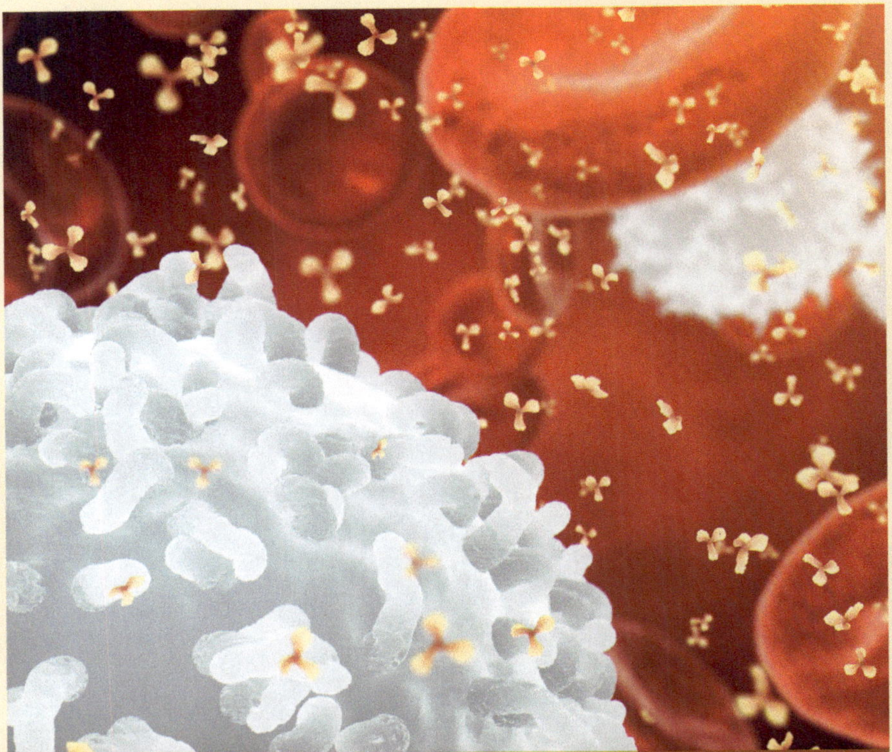

White blood cells called lymphocytes produce antibodies to attack foreign substances such as bacteria.

holes punched in the plumbing of your house. Fluid will gush out of the blood capillaries to cause edema [swelling] in your nose."[5]

Similarly, if the allergen enters the body through the skin, the results are likely to include itching, redness, swelling, and hives. If the allergen enters through the mouth, the lips and tongue often swell. If it enters through the nose, the swelling of the mucous membranes and blood vessels lining the nose and sinuses cause a feeling of stuffiness or inability to breathe. Histamine also stimulates the manufacture and release of mucus, a substance that traps harmful irritants. Depending on where the allergen triggers a reaction, excess mucus can cause a runny nose, watery eyes, or airway congestion.

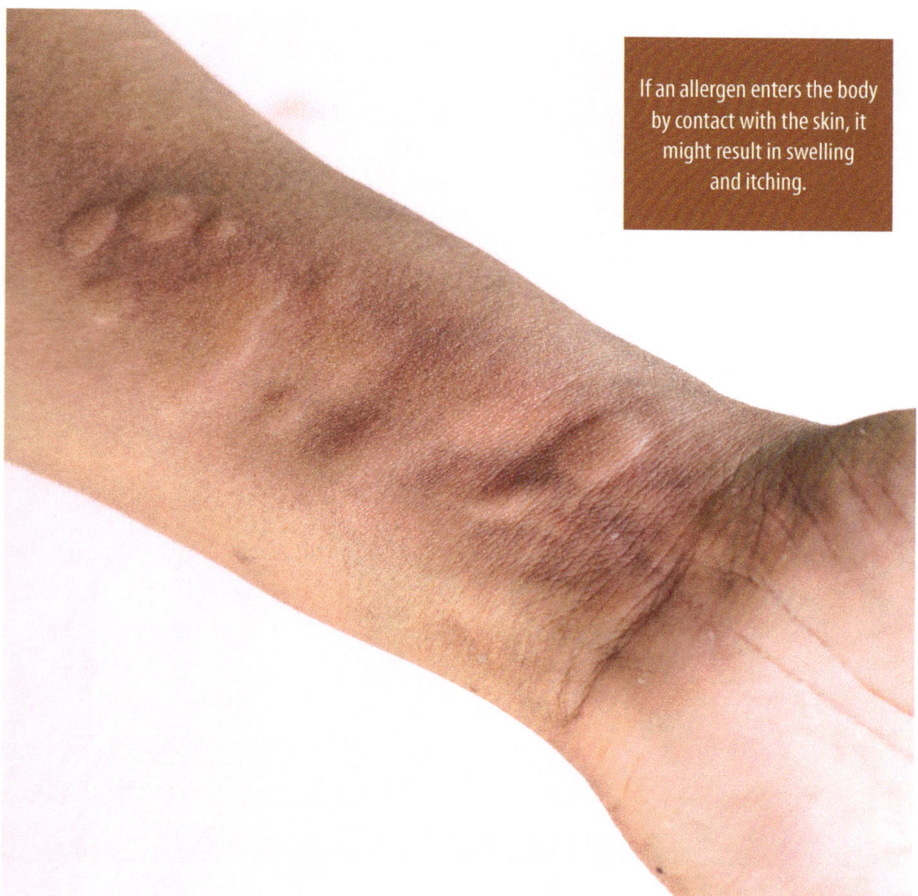

If an allergen enters the body by contact with the skin, it might result in swelling and itching.

Making matters worse, inflammation causes the smooth muscles in the airways to constrict, which leads to wheezing and difficulty breathing. Inflammation also prompts the body to try to expel harmful substances in the form of sneezing, coughing, vomiting, and diarrhea. It is the release of histamine and the accompanying inflammatory response that defines an allergic reaction. It is this reaction, not the allergen itself, that makes people feel ill. John, who is allergic to a number of substances, including ragweed pollen, explained, "Some people can be around ragweed and it doesn't bother them. When I'm around it, it makes me sneeze and my nose run. I know ragweed is harmless, but the way my body reacts to it makes it annoying to me."[6]

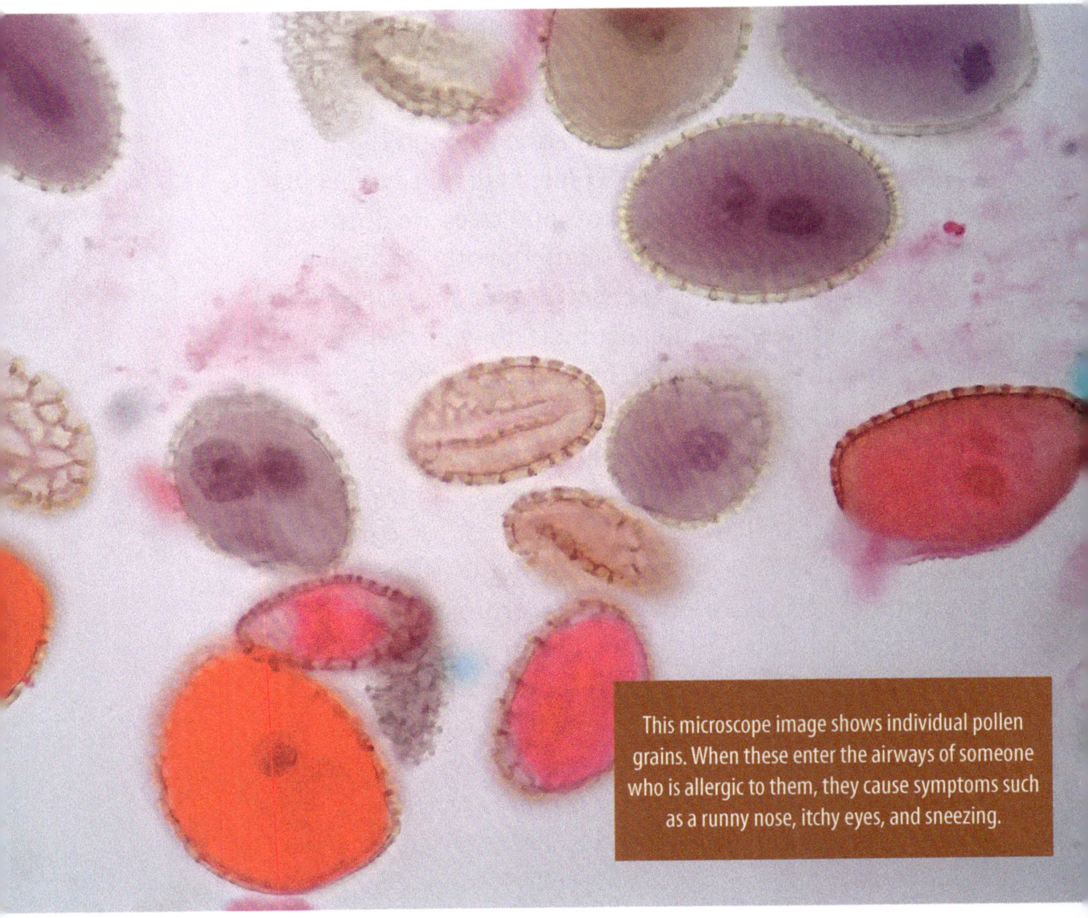

This microscope image shows individual pollen grains. When these enter the airways of someone who is allergic to them, they cause symptoms such as a runny nose, itchy eyes, and sneezing.

Types of Allergens

Inflammation and the problems it causes can be triggered by thousands of different allergens. The body can produce a huge array of IgE antibodies, each specific to a different allergen. Consequently, individuals can be allergic to many different substances.

To make distinguishing between the many different allergens simpler, they are often classified by the way they enter the body: They can be inhaled, be ingested, or enter the body through the skin. Allergens that are inhaled are carried in the air and enter the body through an individual's nose or mouth. They are among the most common substances that trigger an allergic reaction and include plant pollens, mold, dust mites, and pet dander.

Often, pollen allergies are seasonal. In temperate climates, most plants and trees release a high level of pollen into the air during periods of warm weather. The abundance of pollen circulating through the air at this time causes people with pollen allergies to feel ill. During the winter, most plants and trees are dormant and do not release pollen. Consequently, individuals with seasonal allergies feel better then. "As far as my pollen allergies," John explained, "they bother me in June and July. The rest of the year, especially once we get a hard freeze, I hardly notice them."[7]

Seasonal pollen allergies are commonly known as hay fever. Hay fever generally causes allergic rhinitis, or nasal inflammation. It is the most common allergic condition in the United States, affecting an estimated 26 million people. According to Dr. Beth Corn of Mount Sinai Hospital in New York City, "Hay fever is usually what presents in the springtime. And the reason it has this name is because about 150 years ago, the hay harvesting season was in the spring and so people thought the symptoms were from hay. But, in actuality, the symptoms are caused by grass and trees."[8]

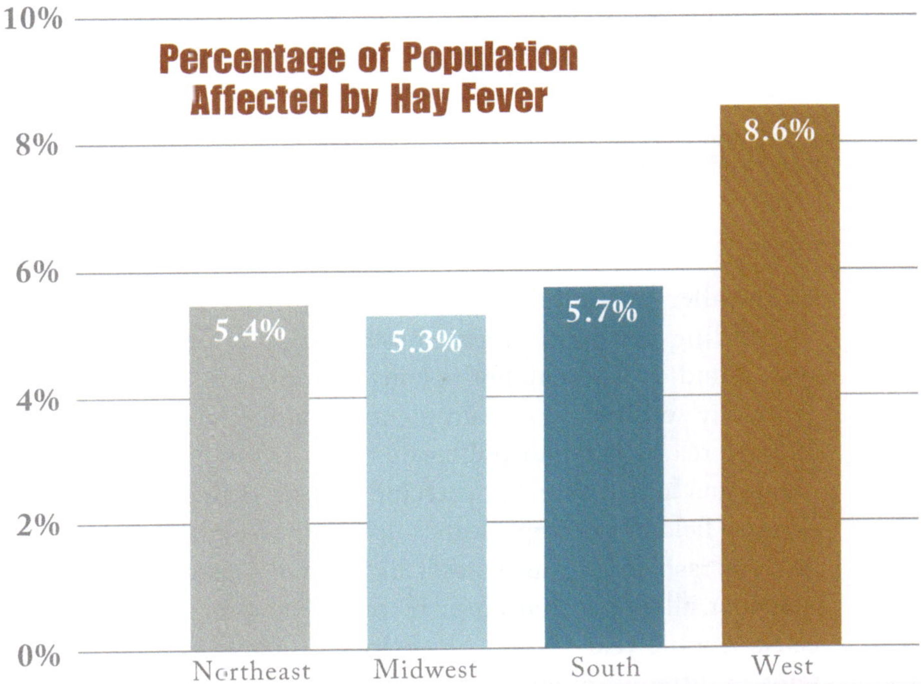

Hay fever affects people in all parts of the continental United States, as this information from the statistics aggregate website Statista shows.

Allergens in the Air

Other inhalant allergens, such as dust or pet dander, affect people year-round because these substances are always circulating in the air. Dust is composed of tiny particles made out of many different substances, any of which can prompt an allergic response. These substances include mold spores and dust mites. The latter are microscopic, spiderlike creatures whose droppings are among the most common allergy triggers. In addition to being found in dust, dust mites live inside pillows, mattresses, curtains, upholstered furniture, and rugs and can be carried around on clothing.

Pet dander is another common allergen. It is made up of proteins found in an animal's (such as a cat's or dog's) saliva, hair, and skin. Pet dander is extremely small. A particle of cat dander can be as small as a half a micron. (One micron is equal to a thousandth of a millimeter.) Pet dander is so tiny that particles of it can hang in unmoving air for up to six hours. The slightest movement gets the particles circulating. Although individuals can be sensitive to all types of pet dander, cat dander allergies are the most common.

Skin Sensitivities

Other allergens enter the body through the skin. Depending on the allergen, these allergies can be year-round or seasonal. For instance, people who are especially sensitive to certain plants may develop an allergic reaction when pollen or resins from these plants touch their skin. For such individuals, sitting in a grassy field, for example, can cause them to develop an itchy rash. Such a response is likely to be seasonal.

Other allergens that enter through the skin can cause trouble year-round. These include latex; proteins in different fibers, such as burlap, wool, or silk; and a wide array of chemicals found in grooming and cleaning products. This is how an allergen in nail polish affected Barbara: "I got this terrible itchy rash on my face, worst of all on my eyelids. It was a reaction to nail polish … It was where I had been touching my face."[9] When allergies cause skin problems such as Barbara's, it is known as allergic dermatitis.

Chemicals contained in insect venom also enter the body through the skin and can cause an allergic reaction in sensitive individuals. Wasps, honeybees, hornets, fire ants, and yellow jackets are the most common stinging insects that people react to. Generally, such stings cause pain, swelling, and itching in the affected area. However, because an insect sting delivers allergens directly into an individual's bloodstream, it can cause a systemic, or full-body, response. Such a response produces inflammation throughout the body and can be potentially life threatening. About 5 percent of people in the United States experience this type of response. Hilary is one of them. She described her response to a bee sting: "I started to itch like mad, all down my body. I felt sick and it was hard to breathe or talk. I went dizzy, and the next thing I knew, I woke up in a hospital."[10] An estimated 90 to 100 people die each year in the United States due to reactions to insect venom.

Common Food and Drug Allergies

Drugs that are administered via injection have a similar effect on highly sensitive people and so do drugs that are ingested. Penicillin and related medications, sulfa drugs, and cephalosporin are frequent allergy triggers, as are aspirin and diphenhydramine.

Certain foods, too, can cause a serious reaction in highly sensitive individuals. Up to 15 million Americans may have food allergies, and they are more likely to affect children than adults. Although allergic reactions to food often involve allergic dermatitis or digestive tract problems, for those who are most sensitive, ingesting or even inhaling a microscopic bit of a particular food can provoke a potentially lethal systemic reaction.

Any food can be an allergen, but peanuts, tree nuts, wheat, milk, eggs, fish, shellfish, and soy are the eight most popular food allergens. They cause 90 percent of all food allergies, with peanuts ranking as the leading cause of food allergies. Moreover, even individuals who do not have food allergies sometimes react to food. This is because certain pollens share similar proteins with certain foods. For instance, ragweed pollen shares similar proteins with watermelons, cantaloupes, and bananas. When individuals who are allergic to ragweed eat these foods, their immune systems may mistake the proteins for that of ragweed and launch an attack. This is more likely to happen if ragweed allergens are also present in the body, or if large quantities of the food are consumed. This type of reaction is known as cross-reactivity. In addition, many fruits, such as peaches, cherries, and apricots, cross-react with each other, so if individuals are allergic to one, they are likely to react to the others as well.

Many of the foods shown here are common allergens.

Genetic Predisposition

No matter the allergen, anyone can develop an allergy. As a result of genetics, some people are more prone to developing allergies than other people. Such people are said to be atopic, which means they are genetically predisposed to developing an allergy. This predisposition is passed down in a person's DNA from parent to child, making the tendency to develop allergies run in families.

Those individuals with a family history of allergies are most at risk. If a child has one parent with an allergy, that child has a 20 to 58 percent chance of also having an allergy. If both parents have an allergy, the number increases to 50 to 80 percent. The variation in the percentages is due to the fact that more than 20 genes are involved in atopy—the condition of being atopic. The more of these genes a person inherits, the greater their susceptibility to allergies. Janey comes from an atopic family. She explained,

> *My father had asthma [a respiratory disorder that is often caused by allergies] as a child, and his sister had it too. In fact she died from it. My mother has never had any allergies, but one of her brothers had terrible hay fever all his life. Out of us four, only my brother, Peter, is completely allergy-free. I had bad eczema [a skin condition associated with allergies] when I was small, as did my sister. So, when our son developed eczema, and then asthma, and an allergy to dust mites that made his nose run all the time, I wasn't entirely surprised.*[11]

Interestingly, although people inherit the tendency to develop allergies, they do not inherit an allergy to a particular substance. Scientists do not know why this is so. According to Dr. Gillian Shepherd at New York's Presbyterian Hospital, "It's an inherited tendency, but you don't specifically inherit an allergy to penicillin, or an allergy to grass pollen. You inherit a general tendency of the immune system to overreact."[12]

What Is Anaphylactic Shock?

When anaphylaxis occurs, shock can follow. During a severe allergic reaction, blood that would normally circulate throughout the body is diverted to and pools in the area where the allergen entered the body. This reduces the amount of blood circulating through the rest of the body. As a result, blood pressure drops.

Blood pressure is created as the heart pumps blood into the arteries, making the artery walls expand. The less blood the heart has to pump, the lower the pressure. With low blood pressure, the heart cannot pump as quickly or with as much force as it normally does. Thus, less blood is pumped to the body. The vital organs become starved for the oxygen and nutrients that blood delivers. As a result, they cannot function properly. If normal blood pressure is not reestablished, the body goes into shock.

Shock is characterized by confusion, weakness, dizziness, a rapid pulse rate caused by the heart beating faster in an effort to raise blood pressure, and rapid breathing, which is the body's way to draw oxygen into the bloodstream. The individual may lose the ability to speak or breathe, or they may become unconscious. If shock is not treated, lack of blood can cause multiple organs to fail. Once this occurs, death follows.

A person can be atopic but not develop allergy symptoms until later in life. Conditions in the immune system are always changing, making it possible for people to develop an allergy or stop reacting to a particular allergen at any point in their lives. In general, food allergies are more common in children than in adults. While hay fever and insect allergies generally make their first appearance during the teen years, drug allergies often develop in middle-aged adults.

Occupational Allergies

Some atopic people live their entire life without developing an allergy, while other people with no family history of allergies develop multiple allergies. Scientists do not know why this is so, but they do know that an individual must be exposed to an allergen for symptoms to arise, and the more intense and frequent the exposure, the more likely it is that an allergy will develop. For this reason, people often develop sensitivities to materials they work with. This is known as an occupational allergy. For instance, bakers are susceptible to allergies to wheat protein in flour, carpenters and sawmill workers to wood dust, hairdressers to dyes and chemicals, hospital workers to latex, and metal-industry workers to substances such as cobalt and nickel. In general, symptoms flare up when sensitive individuals are at work and subside when they leave the work environment. Dale, a physician, explained how an occupational allergy to the powder inside latex gloves affected him: "Whenever anyone in the [operating room] would put on or remove their gloves that powder would fly and I would start to wheeze."[13]

Life-Threatening Allergies

Dale's symptoms became so problematic that they affected his ability to breathe, forcing him to change professions. Indeed, if the inflammatory response that provokes allergy symptoms is not controlled, it can cause a number of health issues. Many people develop secondary conditions as a result. For example, overproduction of mucus can cause blockages in the sinuses, ears, and airways. Bacteria thrive in such an environment, leading to sinus and ear infections.

Asthma is another condition linked to allergies. It occurs when the airways in the lungs become inflamed and constricted, causing breathing problems. About 70 percent of adults with the condition have allergies. Often, the same substances that trigger an allergic reaction will also trigger an asthma attack.

More troubling, if allergy symptoms are severe and worsen rapidly, anaphylaxis can occur. Anaphylaxis is a systemic response to allergens in a person's bloodstream. It is most likely to be caused by food, insect venom, or drug allergens. Anaphylaxis involves the release of histamine and other inflammatory chemicals throughout the body. It generally begins with hives, the swelling of the tongue and throat, and breathing problems. If anaphylaxis is not controlled, it causes a dangerous drop in blood pressure that produces shock.

Shock is a medical emergency caused by the collapse of the circulatory system. If shock is not treated rapidly, death occurs. What makes anaphylaxis especially frightening is that it takes less than an hour from the time an allergen enters an affected individual's body for fatal symptoms to arise.

Although most people with allergies do not experience anaphylaxis, whenever an allergic reaction occurs, the results are unpleasant. The troubling reality is that any number of harmless substances can trigger the immune system to overreact. The inflammation that occurs as a result produces a wide variety of symptoms. For those with severe allergies, the results can be dangerous.

CHAPTER TWO

ALLERGY TESTING AND CONVENTIONAL TREATMENTS

Only a doctor can determine exactly what type of allergies someone may have and how severe they are. Diagnosing allergies involves identifying the particular allergens an individual reacts to. Doctors consider several factors, such as an individual's medical and family history. Some children will undergo allergy testing before they enter school to determine if they are at risk. Testing methods vary based on the type of allergies being tested for. Once the triggering allergen is identified, the doctor will recommend the patient avoid the triggering substance to minimize the need for treatment. When avoidance is not possible, the doctor and patient will work together to determine

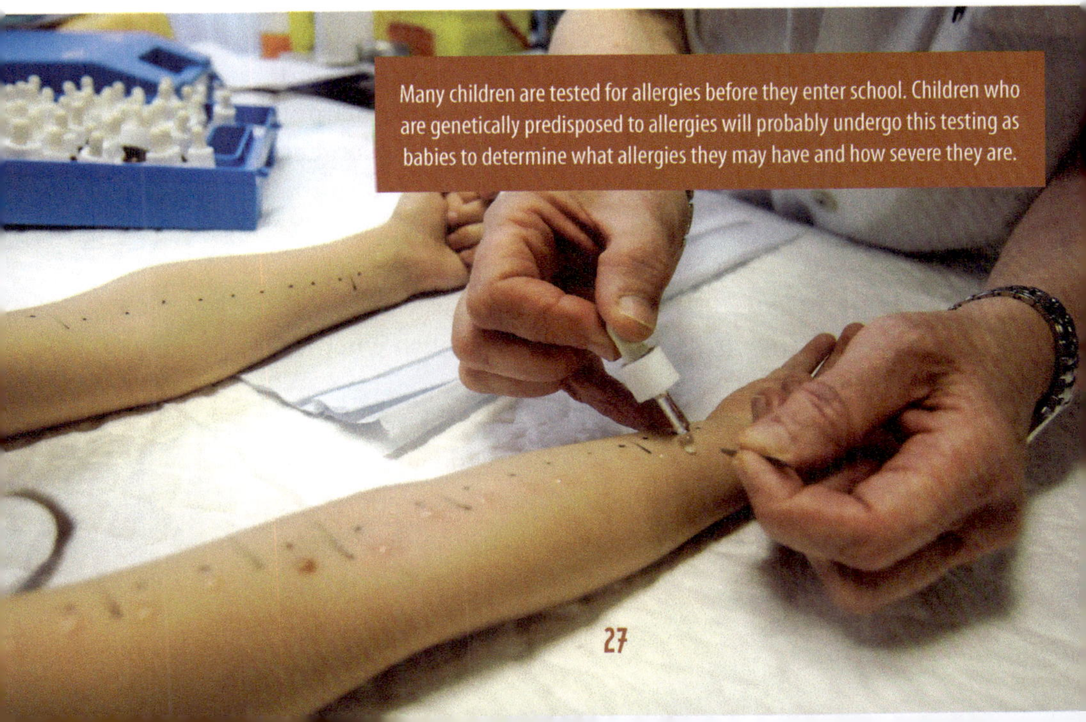

Many children are tested for allergies before they enter school. Children who are genetically predisposed to allergies will probably undergo this testing as babies to determine what allergies they may have and how severe they are.

the best treatment option based on the patient's age, their lifestyle, the substance they are allergic to, and the possible side effects of medications administered.

Identifying Triggers

When a patient complains of allergy symptoms, the doctor must determine whether the problem is an illness, such as a cold, the flu, or a sinus infection—all of which produce symptoms similar to those of an allergy—or whether the problem is indeed an allergy. Administering a physical exam and taking the patient's medical history is the first step. Something as simple as the patient's temperature can help the doctor distinguish between the flu, which causes fever, and an allergy, which generally does not. The duration of the individual's symptoms is also important. Cold and flu symptoms last about a week, but allergy symptoms can persist for months. Patients are also asked whether allergies run in their family. If the answer is yes, the doctor knows the patient is vulnerable to allergies.

If it appears that the problem is an allergy, it is essential to determine the triggering allergen. Once this is known, the patient can take steps to avoid exposure to the substance. When avoidance is not practical, treatment based on the triggering allergens can be administered. Other questions to determine whether the symptoms are associated with a particular activity or time of year—such as eating a certain food, petting a cat, or cutting the grass—help the doctor identify the triggering allergen and establish whether the problem is seasonal or year-round.

Making a diagnosis and identifying the offending allergen in this manner may not provide an accurate picture of the condition. However, if the allergy is seasonal, fairly mild, and not caused by multiple allergens, this type of diagnosis can be effective. According to author and allergy expert Earl Mindell, "You sneeze every time you're near a cat; your throat gets itchy after you eat a peanut; or your eyes start to tear every May at the start of hay fever season. Sometimes figuring out whether you are allergic to something is a 'no brainer.'"[14]

Administering Skin Prick Tests

Sometimes, identifying triggering allergens can be more difficult, especially in cases of year-round or multiple allergies. In these cases, an allergy test is the best diagnostic tool. It can identify which allergens trigger an allergic reaction in affected individuals. According to Katy Weaver, an allergy sufferer and health writer, "It's difficult to find an unfamiliar destination without a road map. It's hard to hit a target unless you know where you are aiming. Likewise, it's hard to find long-term allergy relief without knowing what to change or eliminate. Allergists administer allergy tests so they can have a specific action plan to help you with your allergies."[15]

The most common test is a skin prick or scratch test. It involves exposing the skin to different allergens and then observing the body's reaction. During a skin test, a health care professional applies small drops of diluted, or weakened, extracts of different allergens to tiny scratches on the patient's forearm or upper back. As many as 40 allergens may be applied during one test and may include various plant and tree pollens, mold, dust, pet dander, wood pulp, insect venom, and different foods, to name just a few. The allergens included in the test largely depend on the individuals tested, their medical history, and the types of allergens they are regularly exposed to. For instance, allergy tests in the southwestern United States typically include the pollen extracts of many desert plants. Such pollens, however, are not tested in the Northeast, where the plants that produce them are rare. John, who lives in New Mexico, explained, "Besides being tested for dust and different weeds and grasses, I was tested for mesquite trees, desert willows, and cactus. I was also tested for pecan trees and a bunch of other pollens like chile, cotton, and corn, because they grow in the area."[16]

Before the extracts are applied, the health care professional cleans the patient's skin with alcohol and then makes small marks on the patient's skin. A drop of a different allergen is applied to each mark. Then a small surgical instrument known as a lancet is used to scratch the skin under each drop. This allows the allergen to penetrate the skin. A different lancet is used for each allergen to avoid cross-contamination. Because the lancets are tiny and simply scrape the skin

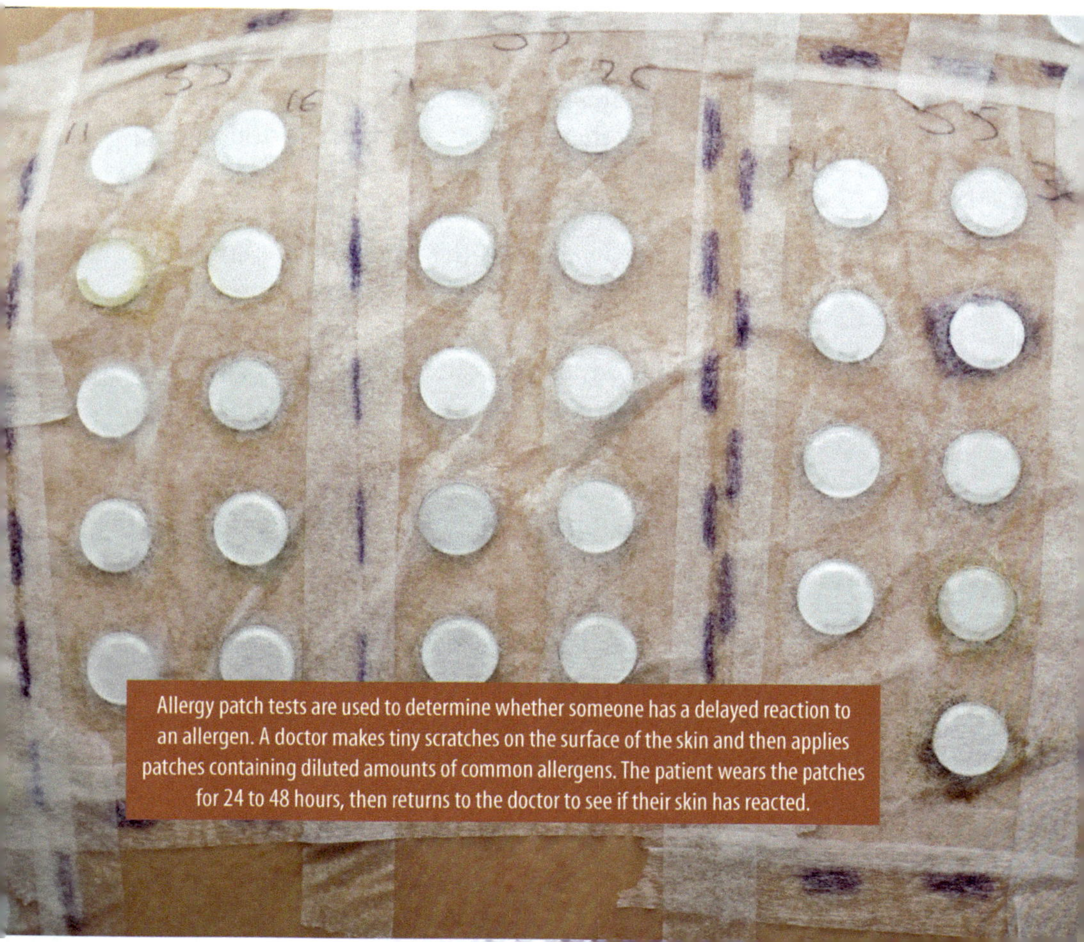

Allergy patch tests are used to determine whether someone has a delayed reaction to an allergen. A doctor makes tiny scratches on the surface of the skin and then applies patches containing diluted amounts of common allergens. The patient wears the patches for 24 to 48 hours, then returns to the doctor to see if their skin has reacted.

without drawing blood, the procedure is not painful.

The allergens are left on the patient's skin for 15 to 30 minutes. Then, the health care professional examines the patient's skin. If the patient is sensitive to a particular allergen, the skin where the allergen was applied will become irritated and swollen, forming a red, itchy bump called a weal. This indicates that the body is producing IgE in response to the allergen. The larger the weal, the stronger the reaction, so the test not only identifies an individual's allergy triggers but also the approximate level of sensitivity to a particular allergen. For this reason, the weals are measured.

Skin tests are effective and show sensitivity even to allergens that are generally inhaled. However, about 50 to 60 percent of skin tests will show "false positive" results, meaning that the patient has a reaction to the prick site even though they are not truly allergic to the substance. In the case of ingested allergens, the body's digestive process breaks food down so thoroughly that proteins that could trigger an allergic reaction become too small for antibodies to detect. For this reason, it may be safe for an individual to consume the allergen even though it irritated their skin during the prick test.

Reactions to skin tests generally clear quickly. However, in cases of severe allergies, reactions can prove dangerous. One in 1,000 allergy skin tests causes anaphylaxis. That is why the tests are always administered in a medical setting under the care of a trained professional who can provide emergency treatment if necessary. In fact, if a severe allergy is suspected, instead of skin testing, patients may be administered a radioallergosorbent test (RAST). This is a test in which a sample of the patient's blood is sent to a laboratory, where a medical professional measures the number of IgE antibodies to specific allergens in the blood sample.

Pollen and Dust in the Air

Television news programs often report pollen counts and dust forecasts, and this information can also be found at any time on the internet. These measurements give the total number of microscopic particles of pollen or dust found in a cubic meter of air in a given day. The number is then given one of five ratings ranging from absent to very high.

The lowest rating is absent. As the name implies, there are no particles per cubic meter that day. A low count is 1 to 10 particles per cubic meter. A moderate count is 11 to 50. A high count is 51 to 500, and a very high count is more than 500 particles per cubic meter.

The severity of an allergy sufferer's symptoms goes up with the rating. At absent and low, most people are untroubled. For sensitive people, symptoms start to appear at moderate. When the rating is high or very high, almost all individuals allergic to that particular pollen develop symptoms.

Windy weather often increases pollen and dust counts, while rain can temporarily wash the particles out of the air. Areas of high pollution, such as densely populated cities, generally experience very high dust levels in the air.

The city of Beijing in China experiences so much pollution that it is often visible. This makes many residents feel sick, and some wear protective face masks to prevent inhalation of the dust and other pollutants in the air.

Testing for Food Allergies

Although both an allergy skin test and a RAST are fairly reliable, neither test is accurate 100 percent of the time. For a number of reasons, including the fact that these tests do not expose patients to allergens in the same way they would encounter them in real life, individuals may not react the same way they do when they encounter the allergen in the environment. For unknown reasons, this is especially true when it comes to foods. If a patient responds positively to a food in a skin or RAST test, many doctors administer a food challenge test to rule out a false positive.

In a controlled setting where emergency medical care is available, patients are given increasingly larger doses of a suspected food. The first dose of the food is tiny. The amount is gradually increased at half-hour intervals until a reaction occurs or the patient consumes a normal amount of the food without reacting. Not only does the test establish exactly what foods a person is allergic to, it also accurately pinpoints the individual's degree of sensitivity to the food. This is especially important in food allergies. Dr. Dan Atkins explained,

> *Some patients or their families become concerned that exposure to even miniscule amounts of a food might cause a life-threatening reaction … These concerns occasionally inhibit participation in normal activities and can lead to social isolation. Although some patients are indeed exquisitely [extremely] sensitive, others find that a larger exposure to the food than was expected can be tolerated without a severe reaction … Alternatively, some patients are found to be more sensitive than was previously suspected and the importance of strict avoidance as well as being thoroughly prepared to treat severe reactions is enforced.*[17]

Antihistamine Medications

Once allergy triggers are identified, patients are advised to avoid contact with the offending allergen whenever possible. If the body is not exposed to the allergen, the immune system will not overreact. Depending on the allergy trigger, this may or may not be reasonable. For instance, people allergic to penicillin can avoid the drug, and people allergic to peanuts can stay away from them. Avoidance is the primary way people with drug or food allergies protect themselves. Avoiding contact with pollen, dust mites, or mold is not as simple. Nor is it feasible for people with multiple allergies to avoid every allergen they react to. In cases when avoidance is not an option, medications that treat allergy symptoms are administered. These include antihistamines, decongestants, eye drops, and nasal sprays, which are most suitable for treating allergies that cause congestion and itching.

Antihistamines are the most common class of drugs used to treat allergies. Generally taken by mouth, antihistamines block the release of histamine, thus inhibiting an allergic reaction. According to Mindell,

> *Histamine works by attaching itself to special sites on cells called receptors. Think of the receptor as a lock and histamine as the key. Histamine unlocks the receptor to begin the allergic cascade that causes allergic symptoms. Antihistamines attach themselves to the same receptors on cells as histamine, which prevents histamine from binding to these sites, thus dampening the allergic response.*[18]

Antihistamines are fast acting, but their effect is short-lived. During allergy season, many individuals take one or more doses every day. Although they do reduce unpleasant allergy symptoms such as itching, swelling, and sneezing, they do not stop them entirely. In addition, many antihistamines have side effects such as drowsiness and dizziness. They can also cause blockages in the lungs of people with asthma.

Despite these health risks, "a medication like Benadryl [a popular antihistamine] remains a powerful and useful anti-allergy medication because it works fast and is quickly absorbed."[19] Antihistamines can also be applied as a topical cream to relieve itchy rashes and in eye drops to counteract red, itchy eyes.

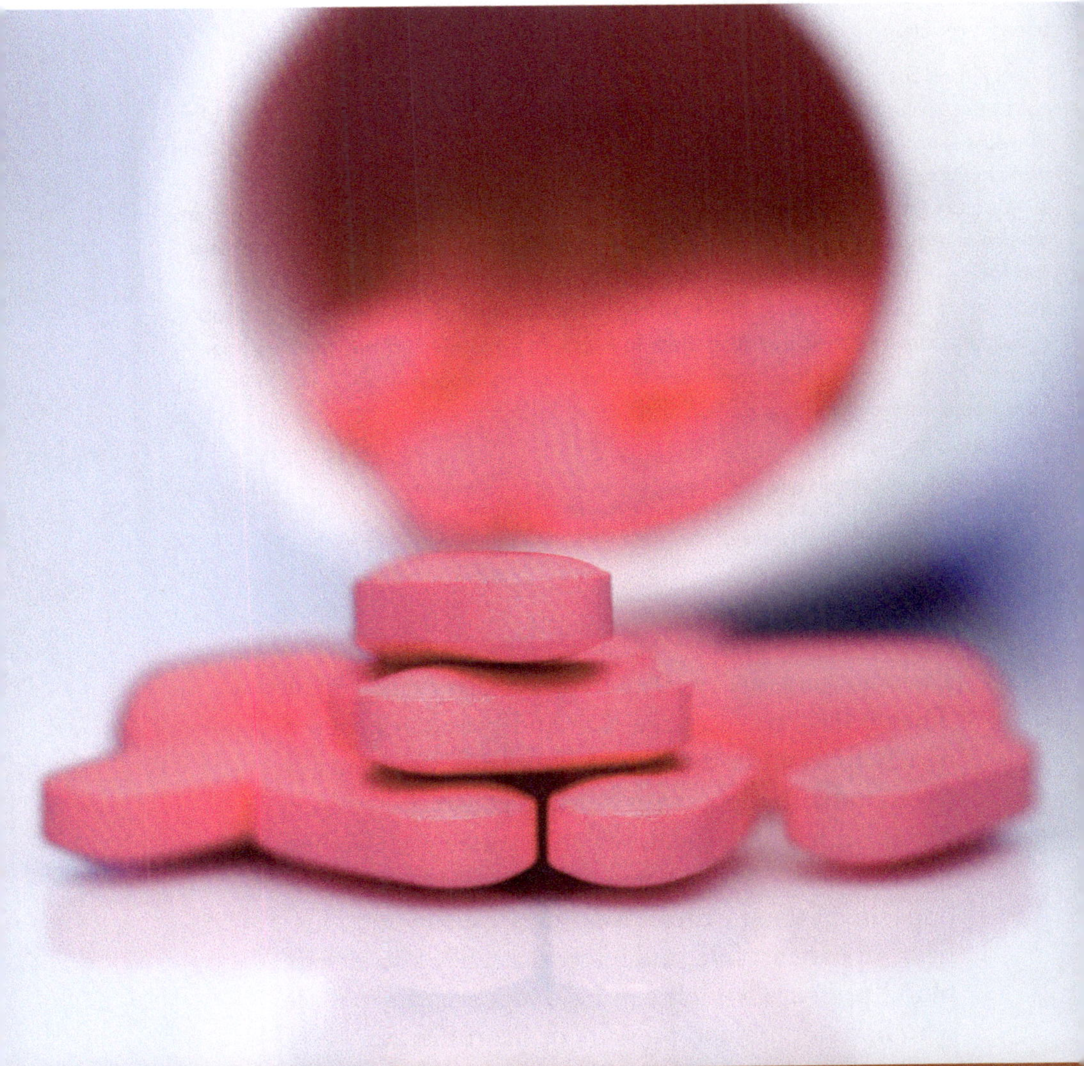

Antihistamines are among the most commonly used tools in the fight against allergies.

Uncommon Allergies

People can be allergic to just about anything, and sometimes allergens can be found in surprising places. For instance, some people are allergic to metals such as nickel and cobalt. This means they may have an allergic reaction to inexpensive jewelry, cell phones, tablets, the buttons on jeans and other pants, eyeglass frames, watches, coins, and zippers. These items can cause a rash wherever they touch the skin. Covering them in some way—for instance, by painting the back of a jeans button with clear nail polish or by using a non-metallic phone case—can generally eliminate the allergic reaction.

In very rare cases, people can also be allergic to things such as water, sunlight, and cold temperatures. An allergy to cold is known as cold urticaria, and it most often appears when someone endures a sudden temperature change, such as putting their arm down on a cold surface or going from a warm room to the cold outdoors in winter. Doctors test for it by holding an ice cube to a patient's skin for five minutes. Another rare allergy is called dermatographia. According to Dr. Kevin McGrath, spokesperson for the American College of Allergy, Asthma, and Immunology, "For these people, even just a tiny bit of trauma to the skin—like the scratch of a fingernail or the rub of a belt or a bra strap—can cause them to break out into hives a few minutes later ... It's not the material or the fabric, but it's the rubbing motion itself."[1] It is important for people to take another person's allergies seriously even if they sound unusual or impossible.

1. Quoted in Amanda Macmillan, "31 Everyday Things You Didn't Know You Could Be Allergic To," Health.com, April 12, 2016. www.health.com/allergy/weird-allergens.

Decongestants and Steroids

Decongestants are another common allergy treatment. They relieve nasal congestion and blockages caused by hay fever and other inhaled allergies. Given orally (by mouth), decongestants work by constricting blood vessels in nasal passages, which reverses the swelling that causes nasal congestion. Their side effects are the opposite of those of antihistamines, causing nervousness, rapid heart rate, and insomnia. They also elevate blood pressure, which can be dangerous for people who have high blood pressure or heart disease.

To lessen the side effects of decongestants and antihistamines, some allergy medications combine the two drugs. Such combinations relieve itching, swelling, sneezing, and congestion without causing drowsiness or nervousness. These medications are available over the counter and in stronger prescription formulas.

Corticosteroids administered as a nasal spray are another way to treat allergic rhinitis. Steroids are man-made copies of inflammation-fighting hormones found in the human body. When the medication is sprayed into the nostrils, it delivers a powerful dose of an anti-inflammatory medication directly to the nasal passages. The medication blocks the inflammatory process, relieving sneezing, nasal discharge, swelling, and congestion. Because it is sprayed directly into the nose rather than taken orally, it does not cause the side effects—such as sleeplessness, indigestion, or dizziness—commonly associated with oral steroid medications. However, nasal corticosteroids can cause a burning sensation in the nose, and they do not produce instant results. Patients must use the medication for several days before seeing a noticeable improvement

Nasal steroids are effective and can be administered at home even to young children. However they do not produce instant results, and they work best when taken before an anticipated allergy season.

in their condition. Full effectiveness can take two to three weeks of daily use. That is why nasal sprays are often combined with antihistamines or decongestants and why many patients with seasonal allergies start using a nasal spray before the allergy season begins.

Immunotherapy Injections

Immunotherapy is another treatment option. In immunotherapy injections, or allergy shots, small amounts of whatever substances an individual is allergic to are injected under the skin. At first, the injected substance is highly diluted so it does not cause an allergic reaction. Each following injection contains a slightly higher dose of the allergen. The goal is to gradually desensitize the immune system to the allergen so it no longer reacts when it is exposed to the substance. Immunotherapy can also be performed by taking sublingual (under the tongue) drops at home. According to the American Academy of Allergy, Asthma, and Immunology (AAAAI),

> *Allergy shots work much like a vaccine. Your body responds to injected amounts of a particular allergen given in increasing doses, eventually developing a resistance and tolerance to it. Allergy shots can lead to decreased, minimal or no allergy symptoms.*[20]

Immunotherapy injections are generally administered once or twice a week for three to six months. This is known as the build-up phase, in which the dosage keeps being increased. Once an effective dose is reached, individuals are given allergy shots once every two to four weeks. This is known as the maintenance phase and, depending on the patient, continues for three to five years or longer. People who take the sublingual drops also continue the therapy for three to five years. The amount of the maintenance dose is determined by the severity of the patient's allergies as measured by the size of the weals in the allergy skin test.

Because thin, small needles are used, immunotherapy injections are not painful but may result in temporary burning or itching at the injection site. According to experts, immunotherapy is currently the best allergy treatment available, especially for people whose symptoms are not controlled with other medications. This includes individuals with severe inhalant allergies, those with year-round allergies who do not want to take allergy medicine every day, and those who want to avoid the unpleasant side effects caused by allergy medication. Results, however, are not immediate. It can take a year before patients notice a significant improvement. Because exposure to even tiny amounts of an allergen can be life threatening to some people, immunotherapy treatments for these individuals must be administered by a physician. Despite these drawbacks, many people find relief through immunotherapy. Sarah, who gets a shot in each arm every other week, explained, "Before I started, I was getting sick all the time. You get to a point when you don't want to live like that. I've been on the shots for a year now and have only been sick once. The shots help a lot. It's worth it."[21] However, even though immunotherapy is proven to be effective, one 2014 study found that most people do not complete the full treatment. According to news website Reuters,

> *Among patients who started the allergen immunotherapy, 40 percent quit before completing three years of treatment and most quit before five years ... Most patients did not give a specific reason for stopping treatment. Others stopped because of the cost of treatment, side effects or lack of benefit. About half of those who stopped taking the drops did so because they didn't like the taste.*[22]

Emergency Treatment for Anaphylaxis

The only treatment for people with food and drug allergies is avoidance. If individuals with severe allergies develop anaphylaxis, urgent treatment is required. Because anaphylaxis can cause shock in less than an hour, it is considered a medical emergency.

Anaphylaxis is treated with antihistamines and epinephrine. Epinephrine is a chemical that narrows blood vessels and causes airway muscles to relax. This causes an individual's blood pressure to rise and relieves breathing problems. In cases of anaphylaxis, quick use of this medication can be life-saving.

Shown here is a woman injecting emergency medication with an auto-injector pen. This medication is easy to administer and works very quickly.

Epinephrine is administered via injection. Most individuals with a history of life-threatening food or insect venom allergies carry at least one auto-injector pen with them at all times. It is a self-injectable dose of epinephrine in a syringe-like device.

Controversy over EpiPen

The most commonly used brand of auto-injector is EpiPen, but controversy has recently surfaced regarding the business practices of Mylan, the company that makes EpiPen. The company has been accused of deliberately increasing the price of EpiPen because it knows people need the medication to save their lives and will be willing to pay a lot of money for it. According to CNBC, EpiPen cost about $90 in 2007, but as of 2017, Mylan had increased the price by 574 percent, making it about $600.

Other auto-injector pens exist and are much cheaper, but Mylan kept EpiPen popular by offering rebates, or discounts, to pharmacy benefit managers (PBMs), who decide which medications health insurance will cover. This has made it hard for other companies to compete with Mylan. CNBC noted, "Most EpiPen customers have some form of insurance that covers all or part of the cost of their purchase … But a small fraction of all consumers pay the list price for the device, either because they have no insurance, or because they are buying multiple packs of EpiPens and only one pack is covered by their health plan."[1] People who cannot afford an EpiPen have to do without it, which is a scary situation for someone with allergies that can cause anaphylaxis. Mylan faced a lawsuit for increasing the cost of EpiPen specifically to increase the company's profits. Legally, companies can increase the cost of a medication only to cover increased costs associated with making the medicine. The lawsuit

> *also claims that CVS Caremark, Express Scripts and Optum Rx "knowingly made material misstatements to health care payers, plan members, and the general public" about the actual price of EpiPen, the extent to which the published price differed from the actual price, and the extent to which they and Mylan "negotiated the rebates discounting the list price of EpiPen for a purpose other than the PBMs' own enrichment."*[2]

In 2017, Mylan settled the lawsuit by paying a fine of $465 million in exchange for being cleared of all charges. This was the only consequence the company received, which has allowed Mylan to keep selling EpiPen at its highly inflated price.

1. Dan Mangan, "Mylan Hit with Racketeering Suit over Big Price Hikes of EpiPen," CNBC, April 3, 2017. www.cnbc.com/2017/04/03/mylan-hit-with-racketeering-suit-over-big-price-hikes-of-epipen.html.

2. Mangan, "Mylan Hit with Racketeering Suit."

A dose is administered by plunging the auto-injector pen into the fleshy part of the thigh. In extremely severe cases, more than one dose may be administered. To make treatment simpler, a "talking" auto-injector called Auvi-Q was released in 2017. When the device is opened, it plays a recording that instructs the user on how to administer the device. According to the CBS network's medical correspondent, Emily Senay, MD, the pen is not difficult to use: "Take it out of the plastic coating, pop off the gray protective top, and put it right into the thigh with force. You want to leave it there for about five to ten seconds, pull it out, [and it] saves your life."[23] A dose lasts no more than 20 minutes, which generally gives individuals enough time to get to a medical facility, where further treatment can be administered.

Allergies, especially severe allergies to foods and drugs, may seem frightening, and people sometimes believe those who suffer from them cannot have a normal life. However, according to experts at the Allergy Authority, a website dedicated to educating the public about allergies, "With more awareness about [allergies] these days and many treatments available, allergy sufferers can find relief from their symptoms so they can enjoy every day all year long."[24]

CHAPTER THREE

ALTERNATIVE MEDICINE AND COMPLEMENTARY TREATMENTS

Alternative treatments are treatments that are not widely accepted by the mainstream medical community in the United States. Unlike conventional doctor's treatments, alternative treatments are not subjected to strict testing by the federal Food and Drug Administration (FDA), a government agency that sets standards for the safe use of drugs. Many alternative treatments undergo limited testing in the United States—although they may be tested and used widely in other countries—and therefore lack enough information to show clearly whether the treatment is safe or effective. Although many alternative health care practitioners go through intensive training, some do not. Some alternative practitioners are not required to undergo years of schooling or take comprehensive licensing exams the way medical doctors are.

Despite the lack of regulation and testing, many health care professionals believe that alternative treatments can be beneficial in treating allergies, especially when they are combined with conventional allergy solutions in a method known as complementary treatment. Such treatments may reduce inflammation, protect patients against secondary infections, and improve a patient's general health and well-being. As a result, individuals gain more control over their allergies. Geoffrey, a family doctor who incorporates complementary treatment in his medical practice, explained, "I think of it in terms of having more tools at our disposal—being able to tackle things from a different angle when standard medicine isn't hitting the spot."[25] Herbal remedies, aromatherapy, nutritional supplements, and acupuncture are among the most popular alternative treatments for allergies.

Why Choose a Different Approach to Treatment?

Conventional allergy medications can cause unpleasant side effects that impact a patient's quality of life. Because they are short-acting, often expensive, and require multiple doses over an extended period of time, many people look for ways to become less dependent on medications.

Immunotherapy, too, has drawbacks. It can take a year to be effective, does not work for everyone, and is costly and time consuming. Also, some individuals are uncomfortable with shots. For these and other reasons, many individuals turn to alternative treatments. As with conventional therapies, the goal is to minimize allergy symptoms. However, despite the fact that alternative treatments are considered to be

Allergies Throughout History

As far as historians know, humans have always suffered from allergies. In 2700 BC, ancient Chinese doctors wrote about using an herb called ephedra to treat plant fever, a term that medical historians say was used to describe hay fever, or seasonal pollen allergies. This treatment is still around today; a drug called ephedrine, which comes from ephedra, is used in modern decongestants.

In ancient Egypt, the early Egyptian pharaoh Menes is believed to have died from anaphylaxis caused by a wasp sting. Inscriptions about wasps are found throughout his tomb. His may be the first recorded death due to an insect sting.

Years later, in about 400 BC, the first case of food allergies was recorded. The ancient Greek doctor Hippocrates reported a case of illness caused by a bad reaction to cheese. From the description, medical historians believe Hippocrates was reporting a food allergy.

gentler and more natural than traditional medical treatments, they, too, are not without risk.

Herbal Remedies

Herbal treatment is an ancient form of medical treatment, dating back thousands of years. It uses the stems, roots, leaves, bark, and seeds of plants known to have healing properties to treat any number of illnesses. At least 25 percent of all conventional medications come from plant sources or contain chemicals that imitate plant compounds. Herbs used to treat allergies contain substances that appear to reduce inflammation. Users say they have a similar effect as antihistamines, relieving nasal congestion, sneezing, and itching.

There are a number of herbs with anti-inflammatory properties. These include garlic, ginger, ginkgo, turmeric, lungwort, licorice, milk thistle, and sarsaparilla, to name a few. These herbs are taken in capsule form or as a tea, either alone or in combination.

Two herbs in particular, butterbur and nettles, have aroused growing interest in the treatment of allergies. Butterbur is a shrub that grows in North America, Europe, and Asia. It has been used to treat asthma, coughs, and headaches for many years. Butterbur contains petasins, which are natural substances that relieve inflammation and relax the smooth muscles in the airways. A 2005 study in Landquart, Switzerland, compared the effect of butterbur extract to equal doses of a traditional antihistamine in 330 patients with nasal allergy symptoms. The researchers found that both treatments provided equal allergy relief. Another study in 2006 in Romanshorn, Switzerland, showed similar results. In that study, 90 percent of the 580 subjects treated with butterbur reported a significant improvement in their symptoms. According to researcher Andreas Schapowal, "Butterbur … is an effective treatment for intermittent allergic rhinitis symptoms and is well tolerated. The effects of this herbal medicine are clear."[26]

Nettles, too, appear to calm inflammation. Leaves from the herb have been used to treat inflammation as far back as ancient Greece. A 1990 study conducted at the National College of Naturopathic Medicine in Portland, Oregon, compared the effect of nettles on 69 individuals with hay fever to that of a placebo, or fake remedy. After one week, 58 percent of the subjects taking nettles reported improvement in their symptoms compared with 37 percent of the placebo group. A few other small studies have produced similar results. However, the herb has not been studied enough for researchers to be able to explain how nettles calm inflammation or to confirm if the herb is indeed effective. Some people may find relief if they use it, but allergy sufferers should beware of products that call it a "miracle cure." Still, many allergy sufferers say that nettles ease their symptoms. Some people take them in pill form, while others use the leaves to make a tea. Nettle products can be found in health food stores as well as some grocery stores.

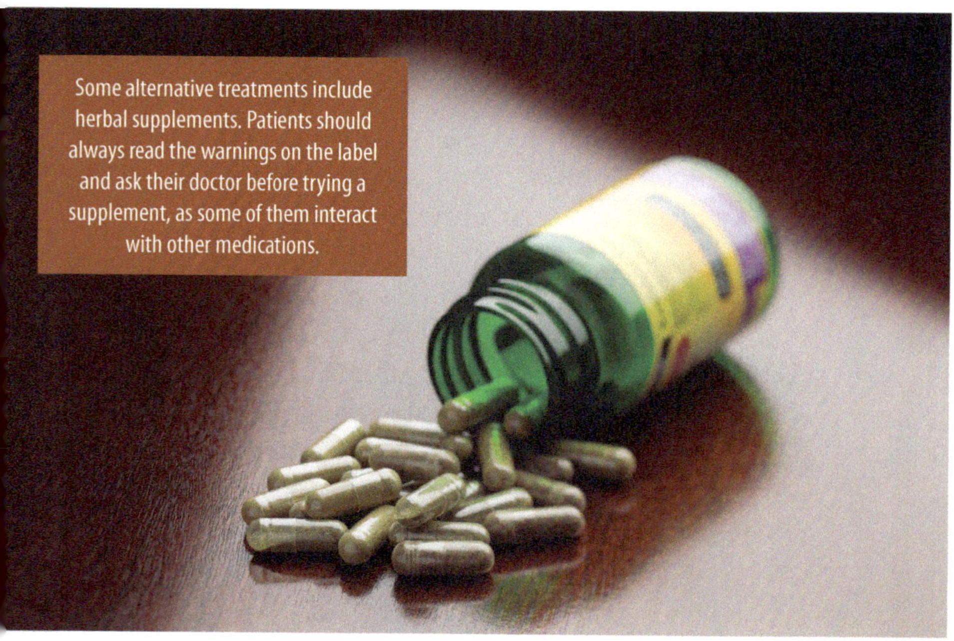

Some alternative treatments include herbal supplements. Patients should always read the warnings on the label and ask their doctor before trying a supplement, as some of them interact with other medications.

Aromatherapy and Nutritional Supplements

Eucalyptus is another ancient treatment for upper respiratory congestion. Rather than taking the herb orally, patients inhale oil extracted from the plant. According to the website Healthline, "Eucalyptus oil is known as an anti-inflammatory and may help you with your congestion. The cooling sensation you experience while breathing it in may also help you feel relief as you combat seasonal allergies."[27]

Oil extracted from the eucalyptus plant can be inhaled to help open the airways and provide temporary relief from mild allergic rhinitis.

Inhaling oils that come from a plant is called aromatherapy. In aromatherapy, oil is generally placed in a special diffuser, vaporizer, or pot of steaming water. There, it heats up and disperses into the air as a mist. Patients inhale the mist into their bloodstream through the lungs. Some aromatherapy is used just for relaxation, but some types are used to treat illnesses. Although there is no definitive proof that aromatherapy is truly effective, many individuals find the therapy soothing. According to Mindell, treating nasal congestion in this manner "helps clear out your airways and relieves congestion without drying out your sinuses, as decongestants often do." Such treatment, he explains, is "old fashioned, but very effective."[28]

While some people turn to herbs, others find that complementing allergy medications with nutritional supplements lessens their symptoms. Vitamins B, C, and E are among the most popular of these supplements. These vitamins are antioxidants—natural substances that help protect the body against damage caused by oxidation, a process in which cells are weakened when they come in contact with oxygen molecules. Cell damage can aggravate allergy symptoms and make the body less able to fight off secondary infections.

Besides being antioxidants, these vitamins have other helpful properties. For instance, all three vitamins appear to have anti-inflammatory qualities. Moreover, vitamin E may reduce the production of IgE antibodies. Some scientists theorize that people with low levels of vitamin E may be more susceptible to allergies. A 2001 study at Aberdeen University in Scotland found that infants born to women who had a diet rich in vitamin E were less sensitive to allergens than those whose mothers consumed less vitamin E. The scientists determined this by performing a RAST on blood taken from the infant's umbilical cord. According to scientist John Harvey, MD, "This is the first study world-wide to have shown an effect of maternal diet during pregnancy on evidence of allergy in the newborn."[29] A follow-up study released in 2016 reported that individuals who supplemented their diets with vitamin E experienced reduced allergic responses to dust and grass.

Regardless of whether these nutrients have anti-inflammatory properties, consuming all three vitamins is an important part of maintaining a healthy diet. It cannot hurt individuals with allergies to add more foods rich in these nutrients to their diet. Good sources of vitamin E include leafy green vegetables and nuts. Vitamin C is found in citrus fruit, berries, peppers, and broccoli. Whole grains, vegetables, eggs, dairy products, meats, and fish are all good sources of vitamin B.

In addition, many alternative health care practitioners suggest that people with allergies add a number of other foods to their diet, such as salmon, cod, tuna, olive oil, nuts, flaxseed, and wheat germ. These foods are rich in omega-3 fatty acids, which appear to naturally inhibit, or reduce, the release of histamines.

Brightly colored fruits and vegetables of all types are also recommended. They contain flavonoids, a group of more than 4,000 substances that are believed to have many health benefits, including anti-inflammatory, antihistamine, and antioxidant properties. According to Mindell,

> *For allergy sufferers, flavonoids can be a godsend. First, they strengthen small blood vessels called capillaries, which help protect cells from foreign particles (such as allergens) by forming a protective barrier. Second, flavonoids reduce inflammation typical of allergies and help normalize immune function, which reduces allergy symptoms. In particular, flavonoids help stabilize mast cells, the*

immune cells that produce histamines when they encounter allergens. Flavonoids calm down these overexcited cells, preventing the release of histamine, which is responsible for those annoying allergy symptoms. Last but not least, by maintaining optimal antioxidant levels in the body, flavonoids help the body cleanse itself of pollution, toxins, and other chemicals that can send the immune system into overdrive and trigger an allergic reaction.[30]

One flavonoid in particular, quercetin, has been the subject of allergy studies. Found in apples, onions, berries, grapes, and green tea, it is chemically similar to a drug used in allergy and asthma medications. Alternative practitioners say quercetin is a powerful antihistamine that also enhances lung health. A University of Nottingham, England, study examined this theory. In the study, which lasted from 1991 to 2000, the lung functions of 2,633 adults who ate at least five apples per week were compared with those who ate fewer apples. The researchers found that those subjects who ate the most apples had significantly better lung function than the other subjects. This means they could exhale air more easily, had less coughing and congestion, and had less severe upper respiratory allergy and asthma symptoms. Another 2000 British study at St. George's Hospital in London yielded similar results. Commenting on these studies, Dianne Hyson, a nutrition researcher with the University of California, Davis Medical Center, said, "This research adds to the growing body of science demonstrating that eating apples may improve health including lung function."[31] For people who want a more concentrated dose of quercetin—for instance, if someone is unable to eat an apple every day—it is available in both pill and powder form. Pills are easier to take and are a better way to keep track of how much someone is taking. Dr. Andrew Weil warns that more than 1 gram per day can cause kidney damage. It can also have severe interactions with drugs that affect the liver, such as corticosteroids, so a doctor should always be consulted before someone adds quercetin to their medical regimen.

Acupuncture

Acupuncture is another alternative treatment that some allergy sufferers find helpful. It is an ancient form of Chinese medicine based on the theory that healthy people have an energy called *qi* (pronounced "chi") flowing through their bodies. If *qi* is blocked, the immune system over- or underreacts, and illnesses and inflammation occur.

Acupuncture involves the insertion of hair-thin needles into specific points in the body where acupuncturists say energy channels are blocked. The insertion of the needles is supposed to open up the channels, allowing the *qi* to flow freely. Since the needles are extremely thin, many people say this procedure is not painful.

Acupuncturists say that once the channel is unblocked, the immune system will return to normal and inflammation will be reduced. Even though many people say that acupuncture treatments have improved their health, there is little evidence in Western science to prove that *qi* exists. Nor have there been many studies on the effectiveness of acupuncture in treating allergies. One of the few is a 2004 study conducted in a Hong Kong allergy clinic that showed promising results. In this study, children with seasonal allergies were divided into two groups. The first group was treated with acupuncture to relieve their allergy symptoms. The second group was treated with what appeared to be acupuncture. In reality, the needles were not inserted deeply enough to be effective.

The second group unknowingly acted as a

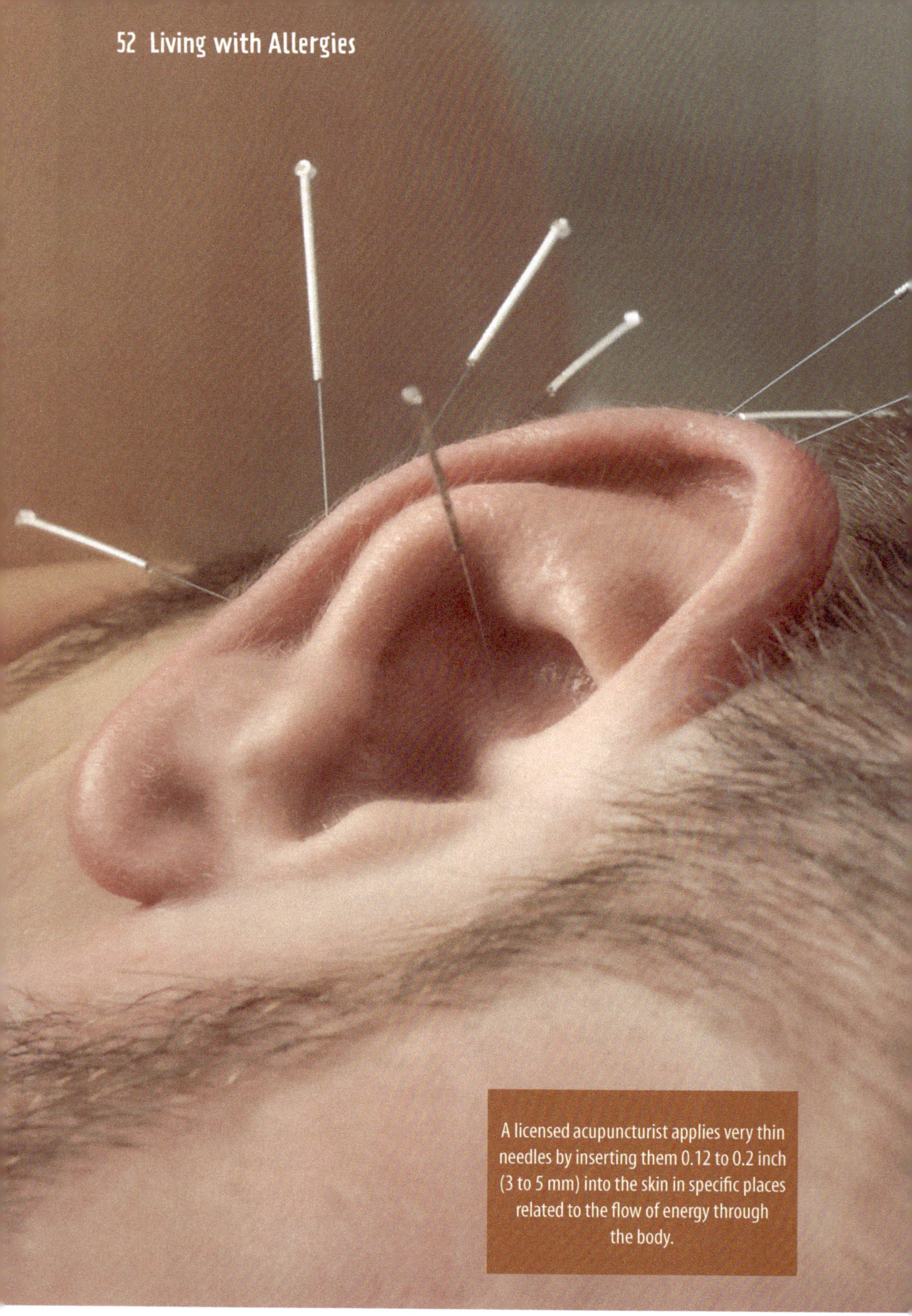

A licensed acupuncturist applies very thin needles by inserting them 0.12 to 0.2 inch (3 to 5 mm) into the skin in specific places related to the flow of energy through the body.

control group, receiving no actual treatment. The real and fake treatments were administered twice a week for eight weeks. The subjects' symptoms were checked daily and scored on a numerical scale. The subjects treated with true acupuncture had lower scores, which translated to fewer allergy symptoms during the treatment period. Moreover, they continued to have fewer allergy symptoms for 10 weeks thereafter. The researchers concluded that "active acupuncture was more effective than sham [fake] acupuncture in decreasing the symptom scores for persistent allergic rhinitis and increasing the symptom-free days."[32]

A similar experiment was performed in Germany in 2013. A group of 422 people ages 16 to 45, all of whom had pollen allergies, was divided into three groups. The first group received acupuncture and antihistamines; the second received sham acupuncture, where the needles were inserted randomly rather than in the approved acupuncture points, as well as antihistamines; and the third group received only antihistamines. Dr. Weil described the results:

After two months of treatment, the researchers found that 71 percent of the patients who received real acupuncture reported improvement in their symptoms and less use of antihistamines than those in the other two groups. However, 56 percent of the patients in group two also reported improvement as a result of the "sham" acupuncture (which they didn't know was a sham). This finding suggests that a strong placebo effect may be at work here.

Four months later, the researchers found that the differences between the groups were less apparent than they had been at first, which may mean that the patients' expectations of acupuncture's effects could have influenced their perception of how well their symptoms had improved.[33]

Although the results seen from acupuncture may have more to do with how someone believes the treatment will work, it is not a dangerous treatment. Someone who finds relief from it may want to continue getting the treatment, regardless of where the improvement comes from. Demand for more research may arise as a greater number of patients seek alternative care methods for their allergies.

Supplementing traditional allergy treatment with acupuncture therapy may help people with allergies. However, it is important to make sure the acupuncturist is a trained professional. Poorly inserted needles can cause pain and bruising, and unclean needles can lead to infection.

Risks of Alternative Treatments

Just as acupuncture administered by an untrained practitioner can cause health issues, other alternative treatments can also cause problems. Herbs, for example, whether ingested or dispersed via aromatherapy, are powerful substances, which, like traditional medications, can cause side effects. Author Linda Gamlin explained,

Herbs produce side effects in just the same way as medicinal drugs do. This is almost inevitable—

> *anything that alters body functions enough to act as a drug will usually have some unwanted effects. In the case of herbal medicines, there is an added complication. Plants contain dozens, even hundreds, of different chemical substances, many of which have no benefits to humans at all—they are just plain toxic. These plant toxins can produce various unpleasant side effects on their own, to add to the side effects of the useful ingredients.*[34]

Nettles, for instance, can cause nausea and an upset stomach. Pregnant women should never take this herb, since it may cause birth defects in a fetus. In addition, it can worsen heart and kidney problems in people with diseases of these organs.

Butterbur also is not without risk. When it is unprocessed, it contains chemicals known as pyrrolizidine alkaloids (PAs). These can cause liver damage and other serious side effects. The National Institutes of Health (NIH) released a report stating that butterbur products that do not contain PAs are safe, effective, and mostly free from side effects. People who report side effects are generally those who are allergic to plants in the daisy family, which butterbur is related to, and the side effects are similar to an allergic reaction. Since the U.S. government does not regulate the purity of herbal substances, it is possible, though unlikely, for butterbur that contains PAs to be sold.

In the absence of governmental regulations, unknown ingredients may also be added to an herbal remedy. According to the National Center for Environmental Health, some herbal products do not contain the ingredients listed on the label and may even contain the very substances individuals are trying to avoid. In 2015, several retail giants in the United States were accused of selling adulterated, or impure, herbal supplements, many of which contained common allergens, such as wheat, without identifying them on the product labels.

Lack of regulations and monitoring also means there is no set dosage for herbal products. Consequently, herbal treatments may be weaker or stronger than patients anticipate. In fact, there have been cases in which herbal treatments have been found to be three times the strength written on the label. This is troubling because some herbs contain substances that are helpful in small amounts but can be poisonous in large doses.

Moreover, since herbs are plants, they can cause an allergic reaction in individuals with pollen allergies. Inhaling essential oils via aromatherapy can also trigger an allergic reaction. Powerful scents can irritate the airways of sensitive individuals, causing nasal congestion and possibly an asthma attack. Even herbal creams can cause trouble. Some contain royal jelly, a substance taken from bees. Such creams can cause anaphylaxis in susceptible individuals.

Nutritional supplements, too, are not without risk. Large doses of vitamins C and E can cause problems such as diarrhea and nausea. High doses of vitamin B3 can cause itchy red skin, while high doses of vitamin B12 can cause an acne-like condition to develop. High doses of vitamin B6 can be even more dangerous, causing numbness and tingling in a person's hands and feet and difficulty walking.

Skin contact with high doses of vitamin E can cause a condition called contact dermatitis, which makes the skin cracked, red, and itchy. Vitamins exist in small amounts in everyone's body and in many foods, and they perform important functions in the body that people need to survive. This means people generally do not have an allergic reaction to a vitamin unless they take it in large doses, such as in a supplement pill. Even if someone gets contact dermatitis from vitamin E, they can still eat foods that contain it. However, they do need to avoid skin products, such as lotion, with vitamin E in them. More troubling, many nutritional supplements contain additives and fillers such as soy oil or cornstarch. If individuals who are allergic to these substances unknowingly ingest them in a vitamin pill, the results can be dangerous. Mindell explained,

> *Therefore, you must read the label carefully before buying any products. Look for products that do not contain artificial flavoring, and if you are allergic to either corn, soy, dairy, yeast, wheat, or gluten, be sure to buy products that specifically state that they do not contain these ingredients. If you are in doubt, call the manufacturer to make sure. If you are highly allergic to a substance, even a small amount of it can trigger symptoms.*[35]

Clearly, alternative treatments can pose health risks and have side effects, just like conventional medical treatments. However, many people with allergies say these treatments help relieve allergy symptoms and enhance their general health, and discussing alternative treatments with a doctor can greatly minimize the risk.

CHAPTER FOUR

LIFE WITH ALLERGIES

Living with allergies is a difficult burden to bear for one's entire life. Aside from the obvious risk they face any time they are exposed to their allergen, those with severe allergies must cope with unpleasant side effects from drugs, inconvenient medical treatments, and sometimes the fear of anaphylactic shock. They must always be prepared with a plan and emergency medication in case they do have a reaction. Such problems can make these individuals feel as though they have lost control of their life. However, they can regain control by taking defensive measures to decrease the possibility of a reaction. Brett, whose son Ben has a food allergy, said,

> *I think about my son's safety every second of every day. It is my top priority and I think a lot of parents don't understand how vigilant you have to be … He has a [plan] that covers the way that the food allergies could impact his learning, and he also has an individual health plan. And the school health aide keeps an eye on Ben and she's aware of how severe his allergy is.*[36]

Household Allergens

Allergy-proofing the home is one way that people with allergies cope. A wide variety of allergens are found in a typical home. These include dust mites, mold, cockroach droppings, and various chemicals. By eliminating or at least reducing their exposure to such substances, even people with multiple allergies can significantly reduce their allergy symptoms. Dr. Pamela A. Georgeson, president of Kenwood Allergy and Asthma Center in Chesterfield Township, Michigan, explained, "When you have indoor allergies, you'll wake up, feel miserable, tired, and your eyes water all the time. It really impacts the quality of life. You don't have to go to extremes, though, to make changes in the home that allow you to live a normal life."[37]

There are many steps individuals can take to reduce allergens in their homes, and there are many products on the market that help clean indoor air. For instance, using an air purifier with a high efficiency particle air (HEPA) filter, which traps allergens, can remove more than 90 percent of allergens from the air. Such a device is especially effective in the bedroom, where dust mites are commonly found. Experts estimate that the average mattress contains more than 2 million dust mites. According to Dr. Heidi Zafra of Philadelphia's St. Christopher's Hospital for Children, "When you shake your pillow and the dust flies, there's excrements from the dust mites, and that's what you inhale, and that's what irritates your nose and lungs."[38]

Covering pillows, mattresses, and box springs with a zippered microfiber cover that repels dust mites can help reduce dust mites in beds. Washing bed linens in hot water once a week also destroys dust mites. Removing bed skirts, fabric headboards, and stuffed animals—all items that attract dust mites— from the bed also helps.

Vacuuming carpets and rugs every day with a vacuum that uses a HEPA filter is another way to defend against allergies. The filter traps the allergens, which a traditional vacuum could otherwise stir up. Rugs and carpets, especially shag carpets, are prime spots for dust mites, pet dander, mold, and other allergens to accumulate.

In fact, some people remove all rugs and carpets entirely and replace them with smooth flooring such as vinyl, wood, or tile in order to completely dislodge dust mites and other allergens. That is what Sarah did. She explained, "I can't live in a bubble, but I try to keep my house as free of the things I am allergic to as I can. I noticed a big difference when I got rid of some of my carpet and put down tile floors. As soon as I can afford it, I plan to pick up the remaining carpet and replace it with wood floors."[39]

Besides vacuuming, frequent housecleaning is another way to reduce household allergens. Reducing clutter, such as piles of newspapers, books, or knick-knacks, reduces places for dust to accumulate. Housecleaning, however, can be problematic for sensitive people. Inhaling cleaning chemicals or dust can trigger an allergic reaction. To solve this problem, some individuals hire a professional housekeeper. If this is not possible, they wear a protective mask that filters out allergens while they clean.

Defending Against Allergens

Using a dehumidifier to dry out household air is another way individuals can fight dust mites and mold, both of which thrive on moisture. Mold frequently grows in bathrooms, kitchens, laundry rooms, and damp basements. Running an exhaust fan in these rooms helps keep them dry, as does fixing leaky pipes, drying bath enclosures after bathing, and avoiding the use of bathroom rugs, which trap mold. Cleaning bathrooms at least once a week with a cleaning agent that contains bleach, which kills mold, is also highly effective.

The leaves and soil of indoor houseplants also accumulate mold, as do the needles of live Christmas trees,

Some allergy sufferers may experience symptoms at certain times of year when they bring plants into their homes. Christmas trees can release microscopic pollen spores into the air, causing holiday-time allergies.

which can also cause problems for those allergic to pine needles. For this reason, many people with mold allergies get rid of houseplants and choose to get an artificial Christmas tree.

Cockroaches are another problematic indoor allergen. They can be found in any building, but they are especially a problem in crowded urban areas where many people live in apartment buildings or row houses. Cracks in attached walls allow the insects to move between residences easily. This is especially true in the South, where cockroaches thrive in the warmth. According to CNN, nine of the top ten roach-infested cities are in the South, although the bugs are not uncommon in the North. A survey by the Census Bureau found that 41 percent of homes in New Orleans, Louisiana, have cockroaches—the highest concentration in the United States. Taking steps to keep an apartment or private home roach-free lessens a person's exposure. Such steps include sealing cracks in the walls, not leaving food out, cleaning up crumbs, and using roach traps. Hiring an exterminator to destroy cockroaches in the home is another possible solution. During the fumigation, and for several hours thereafter, some individuals stay out of their home, since the chemicals used in the process can trigger an allergic reaction in sensitive individuals.

Cockroaches can live almost anywhere, making them difficult to find and remove. Carefully cleaning up food crumbs can prevent roaches from settling in a person's home.

Pet Allergies

Another common allergen found in many homes is pet dander. Although pets are beloved members of many households, pet dander can cause problems for susceptible individuals. As a result, many allergy sufferers make the difficult decision to give up their pets or choose not to get another after one pet dies. "We had two cats," Alan, who is allergic to cat dander, said.

> *Whenever I petted them, then touched my face, my eyes would blow up and water, and my nose would run. I didn't know what caused this. But after both the cats died and the symptoms stopped, I realized I was allergic to cats. I like cats and my wife loves them. Because of my allergy, we didn't get another cat. It was a major and difficult choice.*[40]

Indeed, living without a pet is such a difficult decision that an estimated 75 percent of people advised by a doctor to give up their pets do not do so. Instead, they take a number of steps to keep their allergies under control. Keeping pets outdoors as much as possible is one measure. If pets are allowed in the house, keeping them off upholstered furniture, where pet dander settles, and out of the bedroom helps limit allergen exposure. Bathing the pet with a special shampoo that removes dander also helps. Many individuals limit the amount of time they pet their animals, do not allow them to sit in their laps, and wash their hands frequently.

Some people look for a pet that is hypoallergenic, meaning it does not cause allergies. Some animals, especially certain dog breeds, are marketed as hypoallergenic. However, according to the Mayo Clinic, hypoallergenic pets are a myth:

> *Many people think that pet allergies are caused by a dog's or cat's fur, but the real source of pet allergies is often a protein that's in the saliva and urine of*

dogs and cats. This protein sticks to the dead, dried flakes (dander) from your pet's skin.

Some dog breeds are marketed as hypoallergenic because they don't shed fur or they shed very little. Because these dogs don't shed, the allergy-causing dander that sticks to their fur doesn't get released into the air or onto the floor as much as with a shedding dog. But while you may have less dog hair with a nonshedding dog, no dog breed is hypoallergenic.[41]

Allergens Outdoors

Individuals with pollen allergies face other challenges. Reducing exposure to these allergens is difficult but not impossible. One step many individuals take is to keep their windows and doors closed when pollen counts are high. This is especially helpful at night, since pollen counts peak in the early morning and late evening. According to Dr. Georgeson, "The highest pollen counts are from 4 am to 10 am. You'll wake up feeling symptoms after having a window open all night. You'll wake up with a runny nose and tearing, which is no way to start a day."[42] Using an air conditioner also helps. Window fans, on the other hand, suck in outside air, so many people with pollen allergies avoid them.

Although it is hard to avoid going outdoors, many individuals stay inside on days when pollen counts are high. When they do go outdoors, they often wear a protective mask while gardening or exercising as well as sunglasses to help keep pollen out of the eyes. Once they return home, they can eliminate exposure to pollen that clings to them by changing their clothes, showering, and washing their hair. Another measure these individuals may take is planning vacations to places where pollen counts are typically low. This includes high elevations, the seashore, and many urban areas.

Hygiene Challenges

People who are allergic to chemicals face other challenges. They often develop contact dermatitis in reaction to substances used in personal care products, such as soap, cosmetics, deodorant, hair products, and body lotion. Scratching the rash only causes it to become more inflamed and can break open the skin and lead to an infection. One important step these individuals can take is to avoid scratching. Instead, they can gently massage the area with their hands. They may also apply an antihistamine cream to ease the itching. Wearing loose-fitting clothes that do not rub against the rash also helps keep itchiness down.

Of course, these individuals should also try to avoid exposure to allergy triggers by carefully reading product labels and educating themselves on what to watch out for. They may also try using hypoallergenic products. Such items, which include detergents, cleaning products, cosmetics, and personal care items, are free of perfumes and other chemicals that can trigger an allergic reaction in sensitive individuals. A doctor who worked for Almay, a manufacturer of hypoallergenic cosmetics, explained,

> *Hypoallergenic means less likely to cause an allergic reaction … [Hypoallergenic] products have been formulated and tested to minimize the possibility of an allergic reaction or irritation, making them safe for even the most sensitive skin. Fragrance-free refers to a product that has no added fragrance-masking agents added to alter the product odor … Fragrance is the leading cause of allergic reactions in cosmetics. Products claiming to be hypoallergenic should be free of fragrance.*[43]

People with allergies should look at the ingredient labels on personal hygiene products and household cleaners. Some may be labeled "hypoallergenic," meaning that they do not contain ingredients that are common allergens. However, many products contain "fragrance," which might be artificial or natural. Both can cause allergic reactions.

Living with Food Allergies

People with food allergies do whatever it takes to avoid foods they react to. This can be challenging. It involves not only steering clear of the food itself but also other food items that use the allergen as an ingredient. For example, an individual who is allergic to eggs not only must avoid omelets and boiled eggs but also many cakes, breads, sauces, and noodles, to name just a few of the foods that contain eggs. Common food allergens can also be used in artificial food coloring, preservatives, oils, thickeners, edible starches, and protein powders, among other things.

Diligently reading food labels can help individuals with food allergies to avoid triggering allergens, but this is not easy. Allegra Cullen, who is allergic to peanuts, explained,

> *By the time I was 3, I learned to read my first words. They were nut and peanut. My mom used to write the word peanut on an index card and show it to me over and over again. Then when we were in the kitchen or grocery store, she would hand me food packages like cakes or gravy or potato chips and have me look for the words peanut and nut. But at 3, I certainly couldn't read words like lecithin, mandelonas, food additive 322, hydrolyzed vegetable protein, marzipan and emulsified ingredients, which all contain peanuts or nuts.*[44]

The Food Allergen Labeling Consumer Protection Act (FALCPA), which was enacted in 2006, is helping to make label reading easier for people with food allergies. It requires that manufacturers list any of the eight most common food allergens (peanuts, tree nuts, milk, eggs, wheat, soy, shellfish, and fish) found in a particular product in simple terms on the food label. So, if a food contains the milk protein casein, for instance, the label indicates that the food

The Kiss of Death

In 2006, scientists investigated how long peanuts stay in a person's saliva after they eat. To find out, the scientists had 10 subjects eat a peanut butter sandwich. The scientists then collected samples of the subjects' saliva at different intervals, including after the subjects had brushed their teeth and used mouthwash. Even after brushing their teeth and using mouthwash, all of the subjects had large amounts of peanut residue in their saliva immediately after eating the sandwich. After one hour, six out of seven had almost undetectable traces of the peanuts in their saliva. After four hours, none of the subjects had any detectable trace of the peanuts. As a result of the study, scientists say that people with peanut allergies should wait several hours before kissing someone who has eaten peanuts. Otherwise, they may unknowingly ingest peanut residue or get it on their skin, causing a potentially deadly allergic reaction.

This happened to 20-year-old Myriam Ducre-Lemay in 2012, when she and her boyfriend began kissing after he ate a piece of toast with peanut butter on it. She had not told him about her allergy, and she did not have her EpiPen on her. She died on the way to the hospital. Dr. Christine McCusker, head of pediatric allergy and immunology at Montreal Children's Hospital, had this advice for young adults with allergies after the incident:

> *[This] is why you have to carry your EpiPen, even though you don't want to and even though it's not cool ... The most important part of managing your allergies is that you have to inform people. You have to say, "Listen guys, I have food allergies, I have my EpiPen. If there's a problem, help me." ... People don't necessarily recognize [that] it can go from that point where "I feel funny" to "Uh oh" very fast.*[1]

1. Quoted in Lauren Duca, "This Girl Died from Kissing Her Boyfriend (and a Peanut Allergy)," *Teen Vogue*, June 11, 2016. www.teenvogue.com/story/deathly-peanut-butter-kiss.

New laws require manufacturers to list whether foods contain or were processed with the most common food allergens. Some foods also include clear labeling to show that they are free of certain allergens.

contains casein, a milk product. Many manufacturers also add a warning if the food item is manufactured in a plant where any of the eight major allergens are processed. This is to protect individuals from cross-contamination. Even if a food does not contain a particular allergen, if that allergen is present where the food is prepared, it is possible that cross-contamination can occur via cooking utensils or machinery or if dust containing traces of the allergen settles on the food. For highly sensitive people, even tiny traces of an allergen can be dangerous. For this reason, an individual who is highly allergic to peanuts, for example, will avoid eating a candy bar that is manufactured in a plant that also manufactures peanut candies.

For the same reason, highly sensitive individuals may avoid being seated near people eating something that they are allergic to, since small particles from the food can become airborne and the person with the allergy can inhale them. Moreover, if someone eating the allergen gets it on their hands and then touches something, such as a cafeteria table, and then a sensitive individual comes in contact with the allergen, this can cause a reaction. This is why some students with food allergies eat at a separate cafeteria table or even in a different room from their classmates. Their classmates are often instructed not to bring snacks or party treats that contain the allergen into the classroom. This can be very isolating and embarrassing for the allergic student. Allegra explained that on the first day of school each year,

> *I have to hand in this dreadful note … The teacher stands in front of the whole class and reads this note out loud: "To whom it may concern: Please be advised that Allegra Cullen has a severe peanut and nut allergy. She cannot be exposed to any type of nut or nut ingredient. Please make sure you*

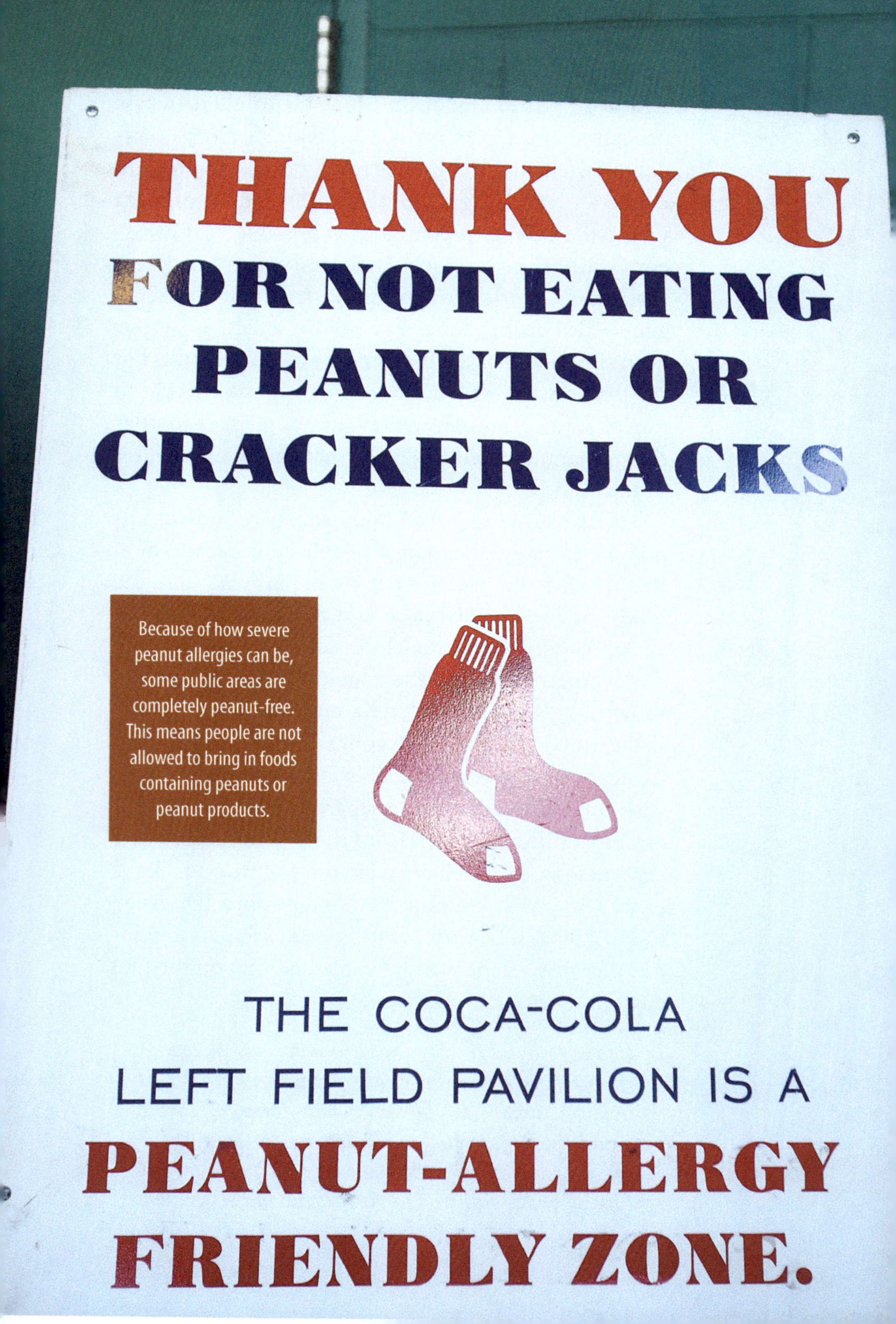

Because of how severe peanut allergies can be, some public areas are completely peanut-free. This means people are not allowed to bring in foods containing peanuts or peanut products.

check all the labels for peanut/nut products or oils. Thank you." I feel so guilty because some kids sigh and say, "Awwwwww"... they know that they can no longer bring anything into the classroom if it has nuts. Then the nurse sends home a note telling the parents, too.[45]

Eating in restaurants or at dinner parties presents more challenges. Unlike food labels, restaurant menus do not list all suspicious ingredients. Individuals with food allergies must question the server about specific ingredients, and many even talk to the chef. Some make up cards listing all their food allergies, which they give to restaurant staff. They also warn their hosts about their allergies before attending dinner parties.

Constantly Prepared

Even when people with severe food allergies and their support networks are careful about avoiding allergens, emergencies can still arise. For them and other highly sensitive individuals, being prepared for an emergency can be the difference between life and death. It also reduces the emotional stress that living with the threat of anaphylaxis causes. These individuals, therefore, carry an auto-injector pen with them at all times. Many also instruct loved ones on how to use the device in case they become too ill to inject themselves.

Some individuals also wear a MedicAlert bracelet or necklace. It is engraved with a medical symbol on the front and a brief description of the person's diagnosis on the back, along with a telephone number. Upon calling the telephone number, which is answered 24 hours a day, first responders are given access to the individual's medical information. This ensures that even if someone is unable to explain what their problem is—for instance, if they are unconscious—medical professionals can administer the proper

A Network of Support

Enlisting the support of others is another way people with allergies cope. Friends, family members, coworkers, teachers, and school personnel all can help allergy sufferers reduce their chances of an allergic reaction. If a severe reaction does occur, their help can save lives. Many teachers, for example, are taught how to administer an auto-injector pen. Teachers and school nurses keep emergency plans on file for highly allergic students. These plans contain contact numbers and emergency care directions. Family members help by not serving foods that a loved one is allergic to. Sometimes this means keeping certain foods out of the house even if they are family favorites.

Airlines, too, are lending support. If someone with an allergy calls ahead of time, some will make special accommodations for them. These accommodations vary from airline to airline. For instance, Delta Air Lines will not serve peanuts on the flight if they are notified at least 48 hours in advance of a person's peanut allergy. If they have less notice than 48 hours, the flight attendants will not serve peanuts to anyone sitting three rows in front of or behind the person with the allergy in an effort to reduce the person's risk of coming into contact with the allergen. The airline will also allow passengers with a nut allergy to board early so they can wipe down their seat and tray table with sanitizer to eliminate any traces of nut that may have been left from previous flights. For these reasons, Delta is known as one of the most accommodating airlines for passengers with peanut allergies.

Many airlines have stopped serving meals that contain peanuts to protect the safety of passengers with allergies, but they cannot guarantee that their prepackaged meals have not been cross-contaminated in the facility where they were made.

treatment as soon as possible. Taking this precaution can help relieve the fear many parents of allergic children face when sending their kids to school or other situations where their parent cannot be with them.

It is clear that when individuals act defensively to reduce the chance of an allergic reaction occurring and to protect themselves if one does occur, they gain control over their lives. As a result, allergy sufferers can live happy, active lives just like people without allergies. Brooke, a teen with food allergies put it this way: "My food allergies are only one part of me; they have never, and will never, control my life."[46]

CHAPTER FIVE

NEW RESEARCH AND FUTURE TREATMENTS

As researchers improve their knowledge and understanding of allergens and how the body responds to them, scientists are working on new ways to help allergy sufferers take control of their allergies and their lives. These include developing new treatments as well as investigating the sequence of events that causes an allergic reaction. Scientists develop theories based on their study of allergic conditions and generally test their theories on animals and human cells before testing them on human subjects. Improvements to allergy control come from both the conventional medical community and the alternative care community.

Scientists all over the world are working on developing treatments for allergies.

Oral Immunotherapy for Food Allergies

Food allergies are one of the most dangerous types of allergies. There are currently few treatments on the market, and many scientists are investigating ways to lessen the threat food allergies pose to susceptible individuals.

Scientists at Duke University in Durham, North Carolina, are at the forefront of this research. They developed and are testing a promising form of oral immunotherapy for food allergies. The goal of the treatment is to desensitize individuals with peanut or egg allergies. However, since injecting even a diluted food allergen directly into a sensitive person's

Duke University in North Carolina is one of the oldest universities in the United States. It is ranked among the top research sites in the country, particularly in regard to the study of allergies.

bloodstream could be disastrous, the scientists developed an oral form of treatment in which patients are fed tiny, but increasing, amounts of the food they are allergic to. Researchers theorize that, as with allergy shots, the subjects' immune systems will eventually build up a tolerance to the food allergen. According to researcher Wesley Burks, MD, "Our goals in treatment are the desensitization, to make them less sensitive and also to make the … allergy go away."[47]

To prove their theory, from 2004 to 2007, the scientists administered oral immunotherapy to 7 children with an egg allergy and 25 children with a peanut allergy in 2 separate studies. Because the therapy is risky, the tests were conducted under tight medical supervision, and the subjects were monitored for hours after each treatment.

Depending on their particular allergy, the subjects were fed tiny amounts of egg powder or peanut flour. The starting dose equaled one three-hundredth of a peanut or one one-thousandth of an egg. The amount was gradually increased until the subjects had some type of reaction. The subjects were then fed a dose just under the reactive dose every day for two weeks. Then, the dosage was increased, and the cycle continued. This procedure continued over a two-year period.

The egg study ended in 2006. At the conclusion of the study, four of the seven children in the egg group were able to eat two eggs without a reaction. The others were able to tolerate less than that amount but more than before they started the therapy.

After 18 months, 6 of the 25 children were able to eat 15 peanuts without a reaction. As of August 2016, results were even more significant. Researchers at Duke were able to successfully treat 80 percent of the children in their study, enough that those children have stopped their treatments and are able to safely eat peanuts without a reaction. "What we're seeing is that they really are less sensitive to peanuts," said Burks.

> *If they accidentally have a bite of something with a peanut in it, they are not reacting ... What we have seen in almost all of them—that they have had mild symptoms the first day or second time and then as you get a higher dose, you get less and less symptoms. That is why we are encouraged by the results so far, because it really does appear that they are becoming desensitized.*[48]

Burks predicts that desensitization will be a treatment for peanut allergies within a few years and that the same treatment should prove successful for other types of food allergies. According to ABC News,

> *The researchers are not the only ones who are encouraged. Jennifer Parks, the mother of one of the test subjects, could not be happier with the results thus far. "It may not make him be able to eat a peanut butter sandwich some day," she said, "but if it could keep him from dying from being in the same room with a peanut butter and jelly sandwich ... just keep him from a life threatening situation, I feel like we won."*[49]

Researching Herbal Medicine

Scientists at Mount Sinai Hospital in New York City are investigating another way to help people with food allergies. By using a mixture of 11 herbs traditionally used in China to fight inflammation, they hope to develop an herbal formula that blocks an anaphylactic reaction. In 2006, the scientists tested the herbal formula, known as food allergy herbal formula (FAHF-2), on mice, with promising results. In this study, 10 mice whose immune system had been altered so that they were allergic to peanuts were administered a daily dose of FAHF-2 for 7 weeks. Another group of 10 peanut-allergic mice acted as a control. Both groups of mice were fed peanut powder monthly. All the mice in the control group developed severe anaphylaxis. The mice treated with FAHF-2 had no reaction even after five weeks. In addition, the mice's blood levels of IgE antibodies and histamine were measured before and after treatment. While the control group's levels remained constant, the treated group's levels declined gradually with treatment and stayed low five weeks after treatment.

By 2015, the same research team, lead by Dr. Xiu-Min Li, was ready to conduct its study on humans. They studied 68 subjects between the ages of 12 and 45 with a history of allergies to peanuts, tree nuts, sesame, fish, or shellfish. Participants were randomly selected to receive either FAHF-2 oral tablets or a placebo (a fake treatment) three times daily for a period of six months. They were instructed to continue avoiding their allergens and refrain from using any other herbal supplements. At the end of the treatment period, the patients were administered a skin prick test containing their allergen. Subjects who showed an improvement in their reaction returned for another administration of allergen three months later, with no further herbal treatment in the meantime.

Unfortunately, while the study showed FAHF-2 to be a safe treatment, it did not prove this herbal medication to be effective at treating allergies in humans. There was no significant improvement over time in the allergic response of the individuals in the study. Many participants also had a difficult time adhering to the three times daily dosage of the medication that was required. The researchers believe that in order for FAHF-2 treatments to be successful, the individuals must be regularly exposed to their allergen while receiving the treatment. Since participants in the human study were instructed to avoid their allergen during treatment, while the mice were administered peanut powder monthly, this variable may have had a significant effect on the outcome of the study. In the future, Dr. Li's team plans to schedule longer treatments using a refined formula that requires the patient to take fewer tablets. They also hope to be able to administer the medication while at the same time giving the participants more frequent allergen exposure.

Injectable Treatments for Food Allergies

While research on oral immunotherapy for individuals with food allergies continues and herbal medications have proved ineffective, development of injectable immunotherapies has been slow and difficult. Researchers at the pharmaceutical company Tanox Inc. in Houston, Texas, developed a bio-engineered antibody known as TNX-901. It is composed of chemically altered IgG, the antibody the body produces to combat almost all foreign invaders. As a result of the alteration, TNX-901 identifies the IgE antibody produced by people who are allergic to peanuts as a foreign invader and blocks it from doing its job. By binding to the IgE antibodies, it keeps them from activating mast cells to release histamine. A widely praised study was conducted on mice and then on human cells with successful results, and since there was no medication like TNX-901 on the market, the FDA fast-tracked the research and development of the drug. During a promising human trial of the treatment, a legal battle occurred between Tanox and its partners Genentech and Novartis over ownership of the drug. This slowed down development, but finally, a medication called omalizumab, sold under the name Xolair, was approved for use in Australia in 2002. Xolair could be administered as injections by the patient at home every two or four weeks. Over the next six years, however, it became apparent that Xolair injections carry the risk of causing anaphylaxis in users with food allergies, and by 2008, it was required to be administered by a physician.

In initial studies, 0.5 percent of Xolair patients developed cancers of the skin, breast, salivary gland, and prostate gland. This prompted a five-year follow-up study to determine whether Xolair was actually the cause of these cancers. As a result of this study, the FDA found that patients treated with Xolair had a slightly higher risk of heart and brain blood vessel problems. In 2014, the FDA stated,

> *Our review of the 5-year safety study found no difference in the rates of cancer between those patients being treated with Xolair and those who were not being treated with Xolair. However, due to limitations in the 5-year study, we cannot rule out the potential risk of cancer with Xolair, so we have added this information to the Warnings and Precautions section of the drug label.*[50]

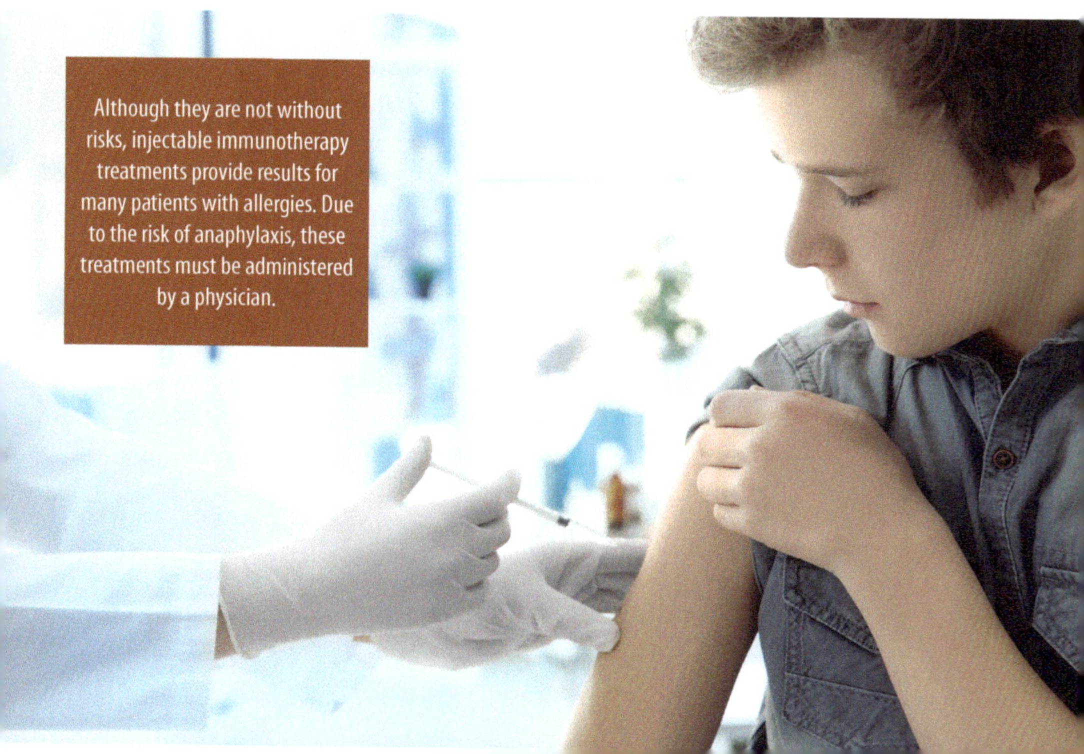

Although they are not without risks, injectable immunotherapy treatments provide results for many patients with allergies. Due to the risk of anaphylaxis, these treatments must be administered by a physician.

Light and Radiation

According to researchers at the Asthma Foundation of Western Australia, exposure to ultraviolet (UV) light may inhibit an allergic reaction. In 2007, the researchers altered the immune systems of laboratory mice in order to give them an allergy. Then, they divided the mice into two groups. One group was exposed to UV light, then to a triggering allergen. The second group, which acted as the control, was exposed to the allergen but not the light. Then, the researchers measured and compared the allergic response in the two groups. The mice that were exposed to UV light had fewer symptoms than the mice not exposed to the light.

Since exposing patients to UV light carries the risk of health problems such as skin cancer, other research is being done on ways to use radiation to treat the allergen instead of the patient. In 2011, scientists in Switzerland used UV light a different way. By exposing shrimp, a common food allergen, to pulses of UV light, they found they could alter the structure of the protein in the shrimp so that IgE in human plasma (the colorless part of blood) was not able to bind to it. Power ultrasound, gamma irradiation, and high hydrostatic pressure have also been used in different methods of altering the structure of allergen proteins in peanuts and soy.

Exposure to the radiation in UV light can be quite dangerous to human beings, so some scientists are working on ways to use radiation to treat food instead of patients.

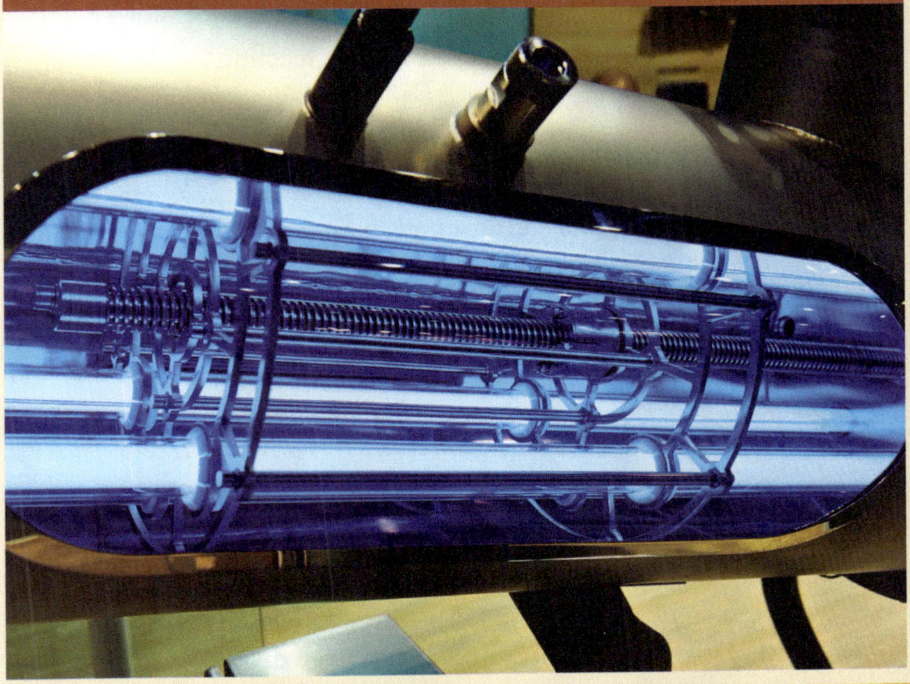

Today, patients ages six and older can visit a doctor for Xolair injections. This is a great benefit to people with life-threatening food allergies. However, there are obvious risks, it does not work for everyone, and when it does work, it takes a long time to see results.

Vaccinating for Allergies

Scientists at Johns Hopkins University School of Medicine in Baltimore, Maryland, are also working on disrupting the sequence of events that leads to an allergic reaction. They are developing a vaccine that blocks the activation of T-helper cells (TH2). To create the vaccine, the scientists used DNA taken from harmless bacteria. Based on other studies, the scientists knew that the bacteria carry a DNA segment that the immune system recognizes as harmless. They theorized that if they created a vaccine that linked ragweed pollen and the DNA, they could trick the immune system into reacting to the bacteria rather than to the pollen. As a result, TH2 cells would not signal the release of IgE, and an allergic reaction would be avoided:

> *The ... vaccine links a ragweed particle to this bacterial DNA sequence. It's supposed to make the immune system of the person with ragweed allergy act just like the immune system of a person without ragweed allergy ... "When this vaccine is injected into a patient, the immune system sees the ragweed component not as ragweed allergen but as [harmless] bacteria," [University of California–San Diego researcher David] Broide tells WebMD. "It calls up the protective immune response instead of the allergic response. So the immune system is being fooled into making the correct response."*[51]

Researchers tested the vaccine in 2006 on 25 adults with ragweed allergies. The subjects were divided into two groups. One group was given one weekly injection of the vaccine every week for six weeks before the ragweed season began. The other group was given a placebo. Once the treatment ended, the subjects kept a detailed log of their allergy symptoms, recording each time they sneezed, their noses ran, or their eyes watered. Compared to the placebo group, the vaccine group experienced 60 percent fewer symptoms. Moreover, although no additional vaccine was administered, in the two years following the study, subjects in the vaccine group were still protected. According to Dr. Peter S. Creticos, the leader of the study, "We can provide relief, very effective relief that lasts for at least a couple of years with a very short treatment regimen. You won't have to take several medicines every day of ragweed season. You won't need shots every week for years. We can turn this disease off for years with a concise six-injection regime."[52]

Creticos calls this type of vaccine "specific allergy immunotherapy" (SIT). It can help patients whose allergies cannot be treated by medications because they are unable to tolerate their medications, or because they have a difficult time remembering to take medications on schedule. Vaccines may be a safer option than conventional allergy shots, in which diluted amounts of the allergen is injected. A vaccine is administered less frequently and does not carry the risk of causing anaphylaxis.

In 2010, researchers in Berlin, Germany, began working on SIT treatments for cat allergies. Using methods similar to those used by the Johns Hopkins scientists, they modified the DNA of feline proteins to create a vaccine. They began a clinical trial to evaluate the safety and effectiveness of the vaccine on people with cat allergies and found that a single dose of the vaccine was safely tolerated by patients. They are currently working on researching the most effective dosage of this vaccine for future clinical trials.

Can Hypnosis Relieve Allergies?

In 2005, a group of scientists at University Hospital in Basel, Switzerland, investigated whether self-hypnosis can decrease allergy symptoms. The study involved two groups of people with hay fever. During hay fever season, both groups were given antihistamine medication. In addition, one group was taught how to hypnotize themselves. While under hypnosis, the subjects imagined themselves in a place free of allergens.

The scientists compared both groups' allergy symptoms over the course of two years. The comparison was based on measuring nasal congestion and the subjects' own analysis of their symptoms. The researchers found that the self-hypnosis group had up to one-third fewer allergy symptoms than the other group. In addition, the hypnosis group needed less medication than the control group.

The researchers are not sure whether the results were actually due to self-hypnotism or because the subjects believed that hypnotism would relieve their symptoms. In any case, the researchers say that since hypnotherapy does not cause side effects, it cannot hurt people with allergies to try it. In fact, there are tapes available that guide people with allergies in self-hypnotism.

Hypnotists put their clients in a deeply relaxed state, in which they are more susceptible to suggestion. They may use cues such as sound, touch, or movement to trigger a state of hypnosis.

Treatments for food allergies, anti-IgE therapies, and an allergy vaccine are just a few of the many new developments in allergy research. According to Dr. Peter Vadas, the director of allergy and immunology at St. Michael's Hospital in Toronto, Canada, when it comes to controlling allergies, "the future looks bright."[53]

NOTES

Introduction: A Life-Threatening Problem

1. "Ellie's Food for Thought," Food Allergy Research & Education, accessed on April 9, 2018. www.foodallergy.org/education-awareness/food-for-thought-video-series.
2. Quoted in Sean Flynn, "What You Can Do About Food Allergies," *Parade Magazine*, April 29, 2007, p. 29.
3. Quoted in "Frequently Asked Questions and Their Answers," Family Allergy Clinic. www.allergiesrus.com/faq.html.
4. Quoted in "Meet Alyssa," The Food Allergy & Anaphylaxis Network. www.faanteen.org/about/alyssa.php.

Chapter One: What Causes Allergies?

5. Frank K. Kwong and Bruce W. Cook, *The Complete Allergy Book*. Naperville, IL: SourceBooks, 2002, p. 102.
6. John, interview by Barbara Sheen, July 25, 2007.
7. John, interview.

8. Quoted in "The Basics of Allergies," Healthology. www.healthology.com/hybrid/hybrid-autodetect.aspx?focus_handle=allergy-information&content_id=1719&brand_name=healthology.

9. Quoted in Linda Gamlin, *The Allergy Bible*. Pleasantville, NY: Reader's Digest, 2001, p. 54.

10. Quoted in Gamlin, *The Allergy Bible*, p. 60.

11. Quoted in Gamlin, *The Allergy Bible*, p. 8.

12. Quoted in "The Basics of Allergies," Healthology.

13. Quoted in Margaret Veach, "Latex Gloves Hand Health Workers a Growing Worry," American Medical News, October 13, 1997. www.latexallergylinks.org/AMNews.html.

Chapter Two: Allergy Testing and Conventional Treatments

14. Earl Mindell, *Earl Mindell's Allergy Bible*. New York, NY: Warner Books, 2003, p. 14.

15. Katy Weaver, "Allergy Testing: Why It's Important and What You Can Learn," *National Allergy*, July 2007.

16. John, interview.

17. Dan Atkins, "Food Challenges: Why Bother?," Atopicderm.org, March 1, 2002. atopicderm.org/news/health-news/y2002/food-challenge-why.aspx.

18. Mindell, *Earl Mindell's Allergy Bible*, p. 243.

19. Kwong and Cook, *The Complete Allergy Book*, p. 127.

20. "Allergy Shots," American Academy of Allergy, Asthma and Immunology, accessed on April 10, 2018. www.aaaai.org/conditions-and-treatments/library/allergy-library/allergy-shots.

21. Sarah, telephone interview by Barbara Sheen, September 26, 2007.

22. Shereen Lehman, "People Don't Usually Complete Allergy Shots or Drops," Reuters, June 4, 2014. www.reuters.com/article/us-allergies-immunotherapy/people-dont-usually-complete-allergy-shots-or-drops-idUSKBN0EF26220140604.

23. Quoted in Tatiana Morales, "Dustin Hoffman to the Rescue," CBS News, July 27, 2004. www.cbsnews.com/stories/2004/07/27/earlyshow/health/main632072.shtml.

24. "The Basics of Allergies," Healthology.

Chapter Three: Alternative Medicine and Complementary Treatments

25. Quoted in Gamlin, *The Allergy Bible*, p. 208.

26. Andreas Schapowal, "Butterbur Ze339 for Treatment of Intermittent Allergic Rhinitis," JAMA Network, December 2004. archotol.ama-assn.org/cgi/reprint/130/12/1381.pdf.

27. "Essential Oils for Allergies," Healthline, accessed on April 10, 2018. www.healthline.com/health/essential-oils-for-allergies.

28. Mindell, *Earl Mindell's Allergy Bible*, pp. 60–61.

29. Quoted in BBC News, "Vitamins Link to Asthma," December 7, 2001. news.bbc.co.uk/1/hi/scotland/1696485.stm.

30. Mindell, *Earl Mindell's Allergy Bible*, p. 66.

31. Quoted in Penn State University College of Medicine Website, "An Apple a Day May Keep the Pulmonologist Away." www.hmc.psu.edu/agromedicine/toolbox/pulmonologist.htm.

32. Daniel K. Ng, et al., "A Double-Blind, Randomized, Placebo-Controlled Trial of Acupuncture for the Treatment of Childhood Persistent Allergic Rhinitis," *Pediatrics*, November 2004, pp. 1242–1247. pediatrics.aappublications.org/cgi/content/full/114/5/1242.

33. Andrew Weil, "Acupuncture for Allergies?," Dr. Weil, May 10, 2016. www.drweil.com/health-wellness/body-mind-spirit/allergy-asthma/acupuncture-for-allergies.

34. Gamlin, *The Allergy Bible*, p. 219.

35. Mindell, *Earl Mindell's Allergy Bible*, p. 26.

Chapter Four: Life with Allergies

36. "Food for Thought: A Day in the Life of a Food Allergy Mom," Food Allergy Research & Education, accessed on April 10, 2018. www.foodallergy.org/education-awareness/food-for-thought-video-series.

37. Quoted in Doug Donaldson, "Allergy-Proof Your Home," *Better Homes and Gardens*, March 2007, pp. 240–242.

38. Quoted in "Living with Indoor Allergies," Healthology, March 3, 2000. www.healthology.com/hybrid/hybrid-autodetect.aspx?focus_handle=allergies&content_id=1723&brand_name=healthology.

39. Sarah, telephone interview.

40. Alan, telephone interview by Barbara Sheen, September 27, 2007.

41. James T C Li, "Are There Any Hypoallergenic Dog Breeds?," Mayo Clinic, October 14, 2016. www.mayoclinic.org/diseases-conditions/pet-allergy/expert-answers/hypoallergenic-dog-breeds/faq-20058425.

42. Quoted in Donaldson, "Allergy-Proof Your Home."

43. "Dermatologist Advice," Almay. www.almay.com/pg/advice/dermatologistadvice.aspx?catid=100006&catnm=ExpertAdvice&subid=7&subnm=Dermatologist.

44. Allegra Cullen, "Guest Columnist Allegra Cullen, Age 12, on Peanut Allergy," Achoo Allergy, accessed on April 11, 2018. www.achooallergy.com/allegra-peanut-allergy.asp.

45. Cullen, "Guest Columnist Allegra Cullen."

46. Brooke Jacobson, "Essay from a Food Allergic Teenager," Food Allergy Initiative, March 16, 2004.

Chapter Five: New Research and Future Treatments

47. Quoted in "Can Deadly Peanut Allergies Be Cured?," ABC News, June 23, 2006. abcnews.go.com/print?id=2107158.

48. Quoted in "Can Deadly Peanut Allergies Be Cured?," ABC News.

49. Quoted in "Can Deadly Peanut Allergies Be Cured?," ABC News.

50. "FDA Drug Safety Communication: FDA Approves Label Change for Asthma Drug Xolair (Omalizumab), Including Describing Slightly Higher Risk of Heart and Brain Adverse Events," U.S. Food and Drug Administration, September 26, 2014. www.fda.gov/Drugs/DrugSafety/ucm414911.htm.

51. Daniel J. DeNoon, "Allergy Vaccine: 6 Shot Cure?," WebMD, October 4, 2006. www.webmd.com/allergies/news/20061004/allergy-vaccine-6-shot-cure?print=true.

52. Quoted in Serena Gordon, "Vaccine May Ease Ragweed Allergies," MedicineNet. www.medicinenet.com/script/main/art.asp?articlekey=76674.

53. Quoted in John Weisnagel, "Peanut Allergy: Where Do We Stand?," Association of Allergists and Immunologists of Quebec. www.allerg.qc.ca/peanutallergy.htm.

GLOSSARY

allergen: A harmless substance, such as pollen or dust, that the body reacts to inappropriately.

allergic dermatitis: Redness, rash, or hives caused by an allergy.

allergic rhinitis: Nasal inflammation caused by an allergy.

anaphylaxis: A severe full-body allergic response that can cause shock and death.

atopy: A genetic predisposition to allergies.

complementary treatment: The practice of supplementing conventional treatments with alternative treatments.

cross-reactivity: A circumstance in which allergens share a similar protein, which causes an allergic reaction to both substances.

flavonoid: Any of a group of healthful substances found in fruits and vegetables.

herbal therapy: Treatment with plants believed to have medicinal properties.

histamine: A chemical produced by the immune system to fight allergens.

inflammation: The body's defense against germs, characterized by swelling, redness, and pain.

lymphocyte: A type of white blood cell that is involved in identifying foreign invaders of the body.

mast cell: A type of cell that lines an individual's nose, bronchial tubes, skin, and gastrointestinal tract.

over-the-counter medication: A drug that can be purchased without a prescription.

placebo: A harmless medication that has no real effects, often used in medical research.

shock: A medical emergency caused by the collapse of the circulatory system.

systemic: Affecting the whole body.

weal: An itchy, red bump similar to a mosquito bite.

ORGANIZATIONS TO CONTACT

American Academy of Allergy, Asthma, and Immunology
555 East Wells Street, Suite 1100
Milwaukee, WI 53202
(414) 272-6071
www.aaaai.org
This professional organization offers information about allergies and asthma, including lists of doctors, allergy news, and an information hotline.

American College of Allergies, Asthma, and Immunology (ACAAI)
85 W. Algonquin Road, Suite 550
Arlington Heights, IL 60005
(847) 427-1200
www.acaai.org
This association provides A-to-Z allergy topic information, lists of allergists, and the latest allergy and asthma news.

Asthma and Allergy Foundation of America
8201 Corporate Drive, Suite 1000
Landover, MD 20785
(800)-7-ASTHMA (727-8462)
www.aafa.org
This foundation offers a wealth of information on allergies, including a multimedia library, links to other websites, pollen scores for major cities, and an allergy glossary.

FOR MORE INFORMATION

Books

Hicks, Terry Allan. *Allergies*. New York, NY: Marshall Cavendish, 2006.
The author of this book gives general information about allergies, including the history of allergies.

Jorgensen, Katrina. *Fearless Food: Allergy-Free Recipes for Kids*. North Mankato, MN: Capstone Young Readers, 2017.
This book gives allergen-free recipes that kids can make and enjoy without worrying.

Ogren, Thomas Leo. *The Allergy-Fighting Garden: Stop Asthma and Allergies with Smart Landscaping*. Berkeley, CA: Ten Speed Press, 2015.
This gardening book teaches readers about what plants to avoid in landscaping and what plants will actually clean the air by trapping pollen and other allergy triggers.

Reino, Jessica. *Food Allergies: The Ultimate Teen Guide*. Lanham, MD: Rowman & Littlefield, 2015.
This book gives allergy sufferers advice on how to gain more control over their lives by advocating for themselves, as well as tips on cooking and living well with dietary restrictions.

Sears, Robert W., and William Sears. *The Allergy Book: Solving Your Family's Nasal Allergies, Asthma, Food Sensitivities, and Related Health and Behavioral Problems*. New York, NY: Little, Brown and Company, 2015.
Written by two pediatricians, this book describes prevention and treatment for allergies.

Websites

Allergic Living
www.allergicliving.com
This online magazine provides tips and information about living with allergies.

Allergy Haven
www.allergyhaven.com
Founded by the mother of a child with food allergies, this website's mission is to educate and empower people who live with food allergies.

Food Allergy Research & Education
www.foodallergy.org
This organization helps connect people with food allergies to a supportive community and is especially helpful for someone who is just learning that they or a loved one has a food allergy.

National Jewish Health
www.nationaljewish.org
This Denver hospital, which is the leading respiratory hospital in the United States, specializes in treating allergies. Its website provides a wealth of information on this subject.

TeensHealth: Allergies
kidshealth.org/en/teens/allergies.html
This website gives an overview of allergies and helpful information, such as how to prepare for an allergy emergency.

INDEX

A

B

C

D

E

F

N

O

P

Q

S

T

PICTURE CREDITS

Cover (main), pp. 52–53, 80 Africa Studio/Shutterstock.com; cover, back cover, pp. 1–6, 11, 15, 24, 27, 32, 36, 41, 43–44, 58, 68, 72, 74, 81, 84, 86, 92, 94–95, 97, 103–104 (orange texture) foxaon1987/Shutterstock.com; back cover (texture) Evannovostro/Shutterstock.com; p. 7 Blend Images—Jose Luis Pelaez Inc/Brand X Pictures/Getty Images; p. 12 Burdun Iliya/Shutterstock.com; p. 14 Alila Medical Media/Shutterstock.com; p. 15 nobeastsofierce/Shutterstock.com; p. 16 chomplearn/Shutterstock.com; p. 17 Choksawatdikorn/Shutterstock.com; p. 22 margouillat photo/Shutterstock.com; p. 27 Daniel Madrigal Madrigal/Shutterstock.com; p. 30 Andy Lidstone/Shutterstock.com; p. 32 testing/Shutterstock.com; p. 35 GIPhotoStock/Image Source/Getty Images; p. 37 grey_and/Shutterstock.com; p. 40 Rob Byron/Shutterstock.com; p. 46 David Smart/Shutterstock.com; p. 47 Alexander Ruiz Acevedo/Shutterstock.com; p. 61 KyleHohler/Shutterstock.com; p. 62 Tevarak/iStock/Thinkstock; p. 66 Nejron Photo/Shutterstock.com; p. 68 Charles Knowles/Shutterstock.com; p. 70 Dina Rudick/The Boston Globe via Getty Images; p. 72 Aureliy/Shutterstock.com; p. 74 Monkey Business Images/Shutterstock.com; p. 75 Bryan Pollard/Shutterstock.com; p. 81 sergeyryzhov/iStock/Thinkstock; p. 84 Voisin/Phanie/Passage/Getty Images.

ABOUT THE AUTHOR

Juliana Burkhart is a native of Buffalo, New York. She teaches and performs acrobatics and hand balancing with a local circus troupe. She is a writer and an artist who enjoys spending free time outdoors hiking and camping.